BRAVING VERACITY

Copyright © 2021 didaink
All rights reserved.

ISBN: 9798730286238

Edited with Stacy Pershall

Introduction written by
Dida Gazoli &
edited by Nancy LaFever

Cover art by Carrie Barcomb

~ for Grace ~

CONTENTS

Editor's Note

By *lidaink*

March 15, 2021

The last 12 months have been some of the most difficult on record since World War II. Living with a life-threatening, public health crisis has given us much to reflect on and write about in 2021. The pandemic also caused many of us to examine other difficult situations in our lives, how we got through them, and the people who influenced us during those times.

Volume 2 of the anthology series is dedicated to the women who changed or inspired us to keep moving through dark days; the women who held the lantern up so we could see the path forward more clearly, and women who faced their own hardships and demons but kept going despite them.

We thank our community of readers in advance for supporting the work of *Braving Veracity* and the courageous women writers who've shared their true stories here. Veracity isn't always easy but it is empowering – it can also be a cathartic way to cope with the isolating and challenging times we face.

Introduction

AMAZING GRACE

By Dida Gazoli

Under the cool swirl of a ceiling fan, I interviewed Grace, an 89-year-old woman from Tennessee with short, silvery-white hair. I was pitching a story to a local magazine about her granddaughter; a dynamic, cutting-edge scientist who lived with multiple physical disabilities.

The temperature was over 100 degrees outside, and I wanted no part of that disorienting heat, even though the blue sky looked cheerful and innocent through the windows. But I knew better. Before I arrived at Grace's house, perimenopause had arrived at my door, and I thought if I had to sit on another porch, I'd leak out the sides of the chair like an oozing, sticky Popsicle. Because Grace was my first official *interviewee*, a Southern-born woman, almost a century old, willing to talk with me at length, I'd try my best to make humidity tolerable, a mental note to get one of those plastic spritzer fans *ASAP*. But I couldn't have been more wrong. Grace couldn't wait to invite me inside.

Introduction

AMAZING GRACE

By Dida Gazoli

"Come in, come in!" she said, "The heat is dadgum awful today!"

"Thank you, ma'am," I said, and lifted my computer bag off my soggy shoulder.

I'd been in the South less than a year in 2010 and had talked with other Southern-born women, but only on their front porches or on the playground of the school my children attended. We'd rented a house in a predominately white neighborhood in Little Rock, Arkansas, and I had yet to meet a neighbor who'd accept my invitation for coffee or lunch. At first, being renters seemed to deem us "transient" or "not worth the time" and my neighbors and I scratched the surface of topics. Our conversations were centered around logistics or grocery stores, BBQ places, family-friendly activities, and Forest Park where our kids went to school together. Then the conversation shifted.

"Where do you go to church?" they asked, followed by, "And what does your husband do? Where does he work?" Once they could see and hear

Introduction

AMAZING GRACE

By Dida Gazoli

that I was not from the South, not one woman asked me anything about myself, the work I did, or where I grew up.

When I did reveal, even though not asked, that I was from California, working on a writing career, and not only was my husband not from the South – he was from *South America*– there was a period of awkward silence. Eventually, they did invite me to join them, just not in their homes, but I was more than welcome to join them at church.

Grace was different. She didn't seem to mind if I went to church or not, where my husband was from or where he worked. If she did mind, she didn't show it.

"Ma'am, can I go through some of the questions I have for you?"

"Oh, please call me Grace," she said. I was *not* expecting that from an 89-year-old Southern woman. I'd heard "ma'am" used while listening to others speak to older women, and I wanted to respect the custom, even if it wasn't my own. But I was also

Introduction

AMAZING GRACE

By Dida Gazoli

relieved that Grace wanted to alleviate the divide between us.

We sat refreshing ourselves under the fan in the living room awhile, and I read through some of my questions. Then we moved to the small kitchen to get something to drink, and Grace described her granddaughter Amanda's childhood.

"Mandy was curious, and always smiling, even after her surgeries," she said, opening the refrigerator door. "You know, she had surgery every year until she was 18. She had a big imagination. Always wanting to be outside, playing in the dirt, and talking to her dinosaurs."

"She talked to dinosaurs?"

"She could see 'em, she said. And maybe she did see 'em. I've seen plenty of things; things I can't explain. You know, she's a horse. The only horse in the family. Full of energy, independent, always chasing after her dreams."

"Do you follow the Chinese zodiac, Grace?" I asked. I was pretty sure she was talking about

Introduction

AMAZING GRACE

By Dida Gazoli

Chinese astrology, but I'd never heard a Southern woman mention it.

"Oh, yes. A psychic told me. She said, 'Honeybunch, you're an only child and were born the year of the dog, 1922.' Oh, I am loyal, always been. I used to think I was psychic too. I knew when Roger would die."

"I'm so sorry, Grace. Was Roger your husband?"

"My son."

She offered me a cold drink in the kitchen, but not the sweet tea I thought she'd serve us. Instead, Grace reached for an ice-cold beer. I had a Diet Coke and sat close enough to hold her hand now and then, while she told me about her son's illnesses and death. Then I typed as fast as I could up another hill of Grace's stories that made my neck sweat – they carried heavy truths and revealed such pain.

"Roger and Mary's father was a dadgum a-hole, and Bob was jealous, and he drank, *he drank*. He made up stories about me, told them I was with other

Introduction

AMAZING GRACE

By Dida Gazoli

men. Whenever he was drinking, he'd look for a reason to pick a fight. Then he'd beat me."

The conversation had veered off in a direction that I didn't think was meant for me. I was trying to interview Grace about her granddaughter, because she was a big part of Amanda's life. I'd never interviewed anyone before, and here was Grace opening up about herself. As hard as the information was to hear, it was also refreshing: *a Southern woman who speaks her mind and reveals her truth.*

Before that day, I'll admit, I didn't exactly trust white women in the South. They said one thing but meant another: "Bless her heart," for example. This was a phrase I heard almost daily from women, but its tone sounded more like a slur than a blessing. Not Grace. She spoke in a tone just the opposite of what her name suggested. And as our time together went on, I realized that 'simple elegance and refined movement' could not tame a woman like her – she was much too free for that. Grace's honest grit gave way to a vulnerability that I liked, and it reached for

Introduction

AMAZING GRACE

By Dida Gazoli

me like a forgotten child. But it's a gamble to listen to such personal things from a woman who says exactly what she means. My first instinct was to duck and cover, cool the fire, change the subject, but I settled in and listened with an open mind. I let Grace feed me another red-hot story about growing up during Prohibition, how her family tried to make money off it during hard times, and how she mostly took care of herself as a girl in the 1920s and '30s. Her words gave me considerable pause, and I would hear them echo in my ears later, like gunshots in the woods. *Could I have survived that life?* I wondered. I didn't think so.

"Roger was as tall as my husband and beat Bob off me one night. Mary threatened her father. She told him, 'you hit me and I'll kill you.' And Bob had a .45 automatic."

"How old was Mary when that happened?" I asked.

"She was in high school, I think. But, you know what? Mary had a good heart. She even taught

Introduction

AMAZING GRACE

By Dida Gazoli

Sunday school at one point. And she loved horses, rode bareback; that's how good she was. And when Bob was doing really bad, he moved in with Mary. She took care of him."

Sometimes Grace's eyes sagged with heavy tears, and the drops would roll past her sunken cheeks. She didn't use her fingers to wipe them away; she used the back of her hand, and I watched her rippled skin smooth out like a crumpled handkerchief under the steam of an iron, even though Grace's fingers were as big and strong as any man's.

Tears pooled like mirrors and her eye color was made bluer, deeper, a shade I'd never seen before – except once, in the cobalt eyes of a childhood friend who told me how much she hated her alcoholic father and what he did to her brother.

The change I witnessed in Grace's eyes invited me in closer, but it was rude of me to stare so long. Eventually, I stopped myself, and said, "We don't have to do this now. I can come back tomorrow." But Grace revved right back up again, as if tears were

Introduction

AMAZING GRACE

By Dida Gazoli

fuel and they'd ignited another memory she was wanted to share.

"Guns weren't toys like they are now. They weren't locked up! They were loaded, dadgummit! A gun was at the ready, and children knew you let it alone. You didn't touch it unless you were set on killing something."

I'd only read about "mamaws" and "papaws" in books, but as Grace described her grandparents, what they meant to her with a sweet tang, the thought of them seemed to sooth her and erased the anger she'd felt moments before.

"Mamaw, she was the steady one. Oh, she ran the show. She was a strong lady and never got TB. She cooked whatever there was and made it tasty. Fish, hog, game, squirrel. My daddy and Papaw kept dogs. Sweet dogs. They didn't come in the house, but they were trusted like family and barked to ward off snakes in the woods and by the river."

During the hours that Grace and I shared those June afternoons, my clammy hands learned to type

Introduction

AMAZING GRACE

By Dida Gazoli

without judgment, my fingers darting across the keys, snatching up what I could from her, pretending I was a real journalist. I wasn't. I was a listener. Still, I wrote down the good, the bad, and the bitter, while Grace turned the pages of her photo albums, and pointed to her children's solemn faces, Amanda's golden curls, her wide eyes and wide open smile, the lemony pajamas she wore in her crib, and her small, amputated leg, wrapped in bandages.

"Mandy was a beautiful, little red baby. She didn't know anything was wrong with her. She was a happy little thing. And my daughter, Mary, was wonderful at that point in time. She didn't complain or feel sorry for herself when she saw Mandy's little leg hanging; she faced the fact – that's exactly what she did. Mandy's daddy, he was wonderful too, but he felt sorry about it, for what Mandy would have to face. He didn't want the doctors to take her leg."

On our last day together, Grace and I laughed and traded a few stories over lunch. I hardly wrote anything down that afternoon, especially when we

Introduction

AMAZING GRACE

By Dida Gazoli

ate in the kitchen. *It might insult Grace if I were to type during lunch,* I thought, *especially after everything she's shared with me.* We'd transitioned from interviewer/interviewee to friends, but I knew it was more than that. Grace had changed my mind about Southern women and the stereotypes I'd believed.

"Oh, I forgot to tell you! Mandy had a horse. Sequoia was its name, like the tree or maybe after the Cherokee Indian, Sequoyah. Mandy would know. Did you know Indians birthed their babies standing up?"

"I did not, Grace. That is amazing."

"Strong women," she said.

Strong women, I thought.

When it was time to go, Grace stood in the doorway and waved goodbye, watching me walk down to my car. I couldn't find any shade on the street and was forced to park in the scorching sun. I looked back at Grace then up into the innocent, robin's-egg blue, sunglasses comforting my eyes.

Introduction

AMAZING GRACE

By Dida Gazoli

Grace had been innocent once-upon-a-time, raised under the same sweltering blue sky, almost 100 years ago, and without any sunglasses to protect her eyes.

On the way home, the air conditioner on full blast in my car, I felt the cold, artificial air soothe my face and neck, and I thought about the day Grace learned to shoot her first gun, "A beautiful .22," she said. She was seven. It was 1929, the beginning of The Great Depression. The same year her mother died.

I drove down a road I'd never been on, through a neighborhood I didn't know. I wanted to see if I could find magnolias still in bloom, but I only saw oak trees lining the streets. Then, in the rear-view mirror, I saw a wiry, brown-haired girl, standing in the middle of the road, under a canopy of branches that blocked the blazing sun. She wore black, army-style shoes without any socks or laces, and a plain white cotton dress. I knew where this girl was headed – into the lush Tennessee woods to look for dinner. She held a jam sandwich in one hand, a gun in the other, her Daddy's yellow dog by her side.

SOFIA'S VOICE

Carrie Barcomb

I pushed the smooth buttons on the phone, and they lit up in gold. Sofia's velvety voice answered. "Hello, dear. I need carrots, potatoes, rutabaga, turnips. Remember, just the freshest ones this time."

I'd called her every day for seven years, just as she asked me to. "Positive thoughts," she'd remind me, decorating every goodbye with, "Until next time, sweetheart."

It was 1991, and I was an 18-year-old college student who'd reluctantly accepted a job as a housekeeper to pay my bills. Each morning, as Sofia chatted in the living room with her group of churchwomen, I washed her marble floors.

I did as she taught me, sweeping the heavy wet mop slowly back and forth, using a mixture of bleach and detergent to create a perfect shine.

"Reflections are essential to increase a home's vitality," Sofia said.

Then one day, she called me into her dimly lit prayer room, where candles illuminated a wooden

SOFIA'S VOICE

Carrie Barcomb

statue of the Madonna, her hands pressed together in prayer.

"What will you do with your life?" Sofia wanted to know. But she would never learn that I finished college and became an artist and mother.

***

Two decades later, I awaken to see what I see every morning: Sofia's cracked but well-loved Pietà, which sits on my dresser in the home I share with my husband and four children.

My phone buzzes with a text from my friend Becky: "Did you start your COVID-19 shopping list?"

Another text, this time from my friend Lauri: "Batteries, toilet paper, dry milk, three-month supply of medications." Unlike Sofia's shopping list, this one feels like an apocalyptic survival guide. She texts again: "Airborne virus, aggressive to lungs, new symptoms: heart attack, stroke. It attacks the nervous system."

"Strengthen your immune health. Stock up on zinc," Donna replied.

SOFIA'S VOICE

Carrie Barcomb

Extremely concerned, I contacted my brother Alan at the federal health agency where he worked as a biologist. His response to my friends' texts surprised me.

"It can be controlled, if we act now," he said. "But I fear our country will be disrupted."

His words still haunt me.

A new world had begun, and I didn't know how long it would take for our lives to return to "normal." But that chat group of local women would soon be my guides, my lifelines.

Strong, civic-minded, and organized, we stuck together in the uncertainty. We started using Zoom to prepare our defense against this new, invisible enemy. I soon learned that Adam, my childhood friend Victoria's brother, contracted the virus and succumbed to it within two weeks. Adam was about my age, and an award-winning musician. Because of hospital restrictions, his devastated family could not be with him when he passed.

SOFIA'S VOICE

Carrie Barcomb

I gave the news to my chat group. Adam was the first person I knew who'd actually died from COVID-19, and his death cemented this new world, showing us that any one of us could be next.

"A lonely death," my friend Kelly said. "I've read that doctors don't know how to treat these patients."

Kelly had moved to Seattle and was now juggling teleworking and managing her children's schoolwork. She shared a story from the San Jose Mercury News: "It attacks the lungs, and victims feel like they're drowning. Patients struggle for air. Blood pressure drops. Kidneys fail. The heart stops."

As we prepared for more lockdowns, grocery store shelves emptied. People started buying toilet paper and eggs from closed restaurants, cars lined up to buy milk directly from farmers, and breweries began making hand sanitizer. Healthcare workers became "essential workers" or "frontline" workers, as if they were fighting a war. According to Brynn in my chat group, nurses were walking off jobs, and those who remained were forced to reuse dirty masks. Another friend, Amy, came within three feet

SOFIA'S VOICE

Carrie Barcomb

of a positive patient at the retirement home where she worked. I didn't know if it would help or not, but I left immune-enhancing vitamins on her front porch.

Our careers and aspirations gave way to domestic work. We joked that this new world would hurt women's empowerment, rendering us voiceless and merely functional. I thought about my mother. She'd once considered herself a "second-class citizen" because she didn't finish college before starting a family. Before she died, I'd complained to her about inequality, and she told me, "Women must learn to work together." Then, in January, before I'd ever heard of COVID-19, my mother spoke to me in a dream. "I'm preparing," she said, walking past me. After I woke up, I thought, *preparing for what?* By March, her message made sense.

My digital network was not only preparing me for the pandemic; they were also preparing and protecting my family, not to mention my sanity. These women lit up my phone each day, alerting me of restaurant closings and COVID hot spots. We analyzed death charts together, and theories about

SOFIA'S VOICE

Carrie Barcomb

how to flatten the curve, and tutorials on making masks. Our hive-mind also kept track of which families had received eviction notices, and which families needed food; we grocery shopped for one another and for families in need, and organized a food co-op. Our sisterhood reminded me that I was not alone. Every morning I went outside for a walk, straining to hear bird calls, kicking trash along the road, clutching my phone and staring into its cool glow, finding new ways to express myself through two-dimensional emojis.

"I can't visit my father," Ashley lamented.

"My brother canceled our upcoming visit," I said.

When May arrived, we watched a rocket launch together online. The rocket, soaring high above the pandemic, reminded us of the awesome potential of technology and humanity. As we watched, I mentioned that my brother was worried about the shortage of carbon dioxide gas (CO_2) in his lab; a necessity, he said, to preserve certain chemicals. He also wasn't feeling well, he'd been working long

SOFIA'S VOICE

Carrie Barcomb

hours, but couldn't get a doctor's appointment until the following week.

That night, I had a dream about a dark cabin high in the mountains. It was snowing outside, and a warm fire glowed in the fireplace. My family, including my mother, waited beside an empty bed. This was the second time my mother appeared to me in a dream, and I was startled by it, awakening moments after it occurred. When I was 25 years old, Sofia said, "Your mother will visit you in your dreams, and you will understand when it happens." But I didn't understand.

The following day, I received news that my brother was gone. A pulmonary embolism took his life after he'd worked until 3:00 a.m. in his lab doing genetic testing -- "To provide answers for a grieving family," he'd said. It was unclear if his death was related to the virus, but his co-worker told me there were several cases within their agency.

I briefly shared my surreal news via text, turned off my notifications, and watched my world shut down.

SOFIA'S VOICE

Carrie Barcomb

I left everything behind and returned to my childhood home for the funeral. I stood in front of masked family and friends, my voice quivering against the roaring wind, my knees shaking, and I eulogized my brother's precious life. Reminders that Mom and Alan were both gone now were everywhere. Then I remembered something else Sofia told me as a young adult, after my mother got sick.

"Focus on others, dear, not yourself. This will heal you," she said.

But the shocking loss of my brother, along with the magnitude of society's growing loss from the pandemic, left me disoriented and yearning for an escape. I wanted to be carefree again, immersed in humble beginnings, and I wanted to totally disconnect from the digital world. I didn't return home right away.

Walking in the woods and reconnecting with nature, I thought about the many things Sofia had shared with me. She was the mother figure a college friend majoring in psychology had pointed out that I

SOFIA'S VOICE

Carrie Barcomb

lacked. At the time, I brushed off the comment, but silently, I thought of Sofia and her influence on me.

Sometimes she squinted her pale blue eyes at me when I was experiencing doubt, and handed me a Bible to read aloud to her. She turned to Psalm 23: *Though I walk through the valley of the shadow of death.* Dressed in a sharp designer dress and classic heels, with her hair pulled back in a jet-black bun, she stood before me like a grand matriarch and said, "These are the purest words in the Bible from God, to lift one's spirit from darkness."

I thought of my brother and his life's work as a public health biologist, and my mother's career as a social worker, devoted to welfare mothers, orphans and foster families. And I thought about some of the last things Sofia told me. The month before I polished her floors for the last time, she mentioned that her work with me was done. Seven years earlier, when we met, she expressed that she worried I might end up on the streets unless I worked for her. At 18, I knew I was lost, but I also didn't know what exactly

SOFIA'S VOICE

Carrie Barcomb

this powerful woman was trying to tell me. She led me to her prayer room one last time.

"You just have to think of me and everything I've taught you. Find and trust the women in your life. *Anon to God*," Sofia said. *Give directly to God.*

A month later, I showed up for work to an empty house. She'd vanished. Sitting where my water bucket normally sat was the small statue of *La Madonna della Pietá*. I picked up the Pietà and took it with me. Sofia left no note and never explained why she packed up and left without any explanation.

***

I was finally able to return home. Approaching my house, I turned on my phone and listened to friends' messages. They'd been preparing for my arrival, dropping off food on my doorstep.

I parked my car and straightened the necklace Sofia gave me. She said to always keep it with me, so I wear it or keep it in my purse. Since the

day.

ne. It

wn as

SOFIA'S VOICE

Carrie Barcomb

the "Little Flower," who died of tuberculosis at the age of twenty-four.

I walked past fallen leaves, with sunshine streaming through the tree canopy, illuminating warm reds and oranges like stained glass, and arrived at my house. My porch overflowed with baskets and sunflowers. The smell of cinnamon, nutmeg, banana, fresh muffins and breads, pumpkin donuts, and homemade vegetarian chili filled the air with hope. Handwritten notes were attached to the baskets.

"When you're grieving, you need some sugar to give you energy," one said.

"We miss you and love you always," said another.

Positive thoughts, I heard Sofia say.

I unwrapped a warm blueberry muffin and turned my group notifications back on.

I CALLED HER GINYA

Catherine Braik-Selin

If I close my eyes, I can leave my body. I float beneath the ceiling and look down, down, down, anywhere but the bed with its scratchy, olive brown army blanket. I see flashes of black and white limbs. I am flying, just like Mary Poppins, around and around. Mary Poppins is my favorite, especially when she jumped into a painting at the sidewalk art show, and *boom!* There she was in Paris, singing in the rain beneath the Eiffel Tower.

I try not to look down while Michael is doing it to me, so I drift along like a puffy cloud and sing happy songs in my head.

Let's go fly a kite, up to the highest height!
Just a spoonful of sugar helps the medicine go down!
Supercalifragilisticexpialidocius!
Chim chiminey, Chim chiminey,
Chim chim cher-ee!

I CALLED HER GINYA

Catherine Braik-Selin

The only part of my body I can still feel are my fingers, which tap a lively rhythm at my sides, along with the melodies. When Michael is done, the songs abruptly stop, and I crash down into my little white, seven-year-old body with its raw, sticky places. Quietly, I pad down each stair to the bathroom, tiptoeing past my parents' bedroom door. I want to go in and curl up next to my father, but I know that if I wake my mother, she'll send me back to bed.

I imagine her saying, "Cathy, you little pest! Leave us alone," and I quietly lock the bathroom door instead and take comfort in the feel of the cool black and white tiles underfoot. The warm, soapy washcloth makes me feel clean on the outside, but it can never erase the dirty secrets I must keep.

Shame grows in the pit of my stomach like one of the knotty galls on our old maple tree, a crusty blemish, an aberration of nature. I become convinced people can see it inside of me, as if they're wearing those X-ray glasses advertised in the back of the

I CALLED HER GINYA

Catherine Braik-Selin

Archie comics I buy at the Sweet Shoppe with my allowance.

***

Michael enters my room silently on the evenings when his mother, Virginia, our live-in maid, goes out on the town with Bob in his Chevy Bel Air. I cry and tug on her skirt. "Please, Ginya, please don't go. Stay with me!" I beg, up until the very moment she steps into the passenger seat and latches the door.

"Now, now, honey child, your Ginya will be back real soon. Stop all that fussing and run along," she reassures me as she rolls up the window. The car pulls away from the curb. When she is gone, Michael plays The Rolling Stones' album *Paint It Black* with the volume turned way up, pounding on his drums, and singing along, "I see a red door and I want to paint it black. No colors anymore, I want it to turn black."

Later, I will make a scene in the TV room. My mother will be well into her bottle of sherry by then, and my father behind the closed bedroom door,

I CALLED HER GINYA

Catherine Braik-Selin

puffing away on his oxygen tank, too sick to hear me pleading for one more show in the hopes that Ginya will come home before Michael can get me. Michael will be sitting in the TV room, giving me threatening glances from the other end of the couch.

On the weekends, I act out in every imaginable way to get my parents' attention, short of actually tattling on Michael, who I know will hurt me *real bad* if I do, like when he showed off to his friend and stood on my head as I lay on the TV-room floor. Even though he put a pillow on top, I was sure my head would split open like a ripe cantaloupe. Night after dreaded night, I failed to escape the dark shadow next to my bed, tugging on my nightgown until I followed him into his room ever-so-quietly.

Wish upon a star, blow the candles on my birthday cake, ask the Magic 8-ball, throw a penny in the pool – my wish is always the same. I imagine hiding in a locked metal box under my bed where Michael can't get me. Only in my dark fortress will I

I CALLED HER GINYA

Catherine Braik-Selin

be safe until morning, holding the key tightly in my hand.

When morning finally dawns, there will be warm Cream of Wheat with brown sugar on top waiting for me at the breakfast table. After school, I'll fill my pockets with glossy brown chestnuts, cracked free from their thick, spiked shells, the color of inchworms. When I return home, Ginya will be ironing in the dining room with a glass of lemonade and the radio on. Her ample bosom, soft, round cheeks, warm eyes and arms will enfold me. I'll breathe in the scent of her honeyed skin and freshly ironed cotton and then, only then, will I be entirely safe.

***

Two years earlier – in my "before" – there was no Michael. I never once heard his name. I had no idea that Ginya was anyone's mama before she lived with us. But not long after my fifth birthday in 1963, the radiator clanking in time with a bare tree branch tapping on the window in the TV room, the windows

I CALLED HER GINYA

Catherine Braik-Selin

of my child playhouse were also shaking, the outside world crashing in.

That morning I'd smelled Ginya's peanut butter cookies baking. I bounded down the stairs and into the kitchen, and practically stopped midair –my precious Ginya sat slumped over the kitchen table, her head in her hands, while my baby brother Charlie fussed in his playpen nearby.

"Oh, Lordy, Lordy," she muttered, shaking her head with a steady stream of *uh-hmms* and *tsk-tsks*. The news was blaring from the radio but my noisy intrusion had awakened Ginya from her haze of grief, and just in time to rescue the last batch of cookies from burning.

"Ginya, why are you so sad?" I asked.

"Honey, the president just got shot and killed. You better run out and wait for your sisters. They done shut down all the schools."

I grabbed a handful of warm cookies and ran out the door and through the swirling autumn leaves, kicking up acorns all the way to the overgrown hedge

I CALLED HER GINYA

Catherine Braik-Selin

along Blanch Avenue. When I found my Ginya like that, I felt her tears spill over and into my eyes. It was the first time I ever saw a grown-up cry.

Pacing back and forth from the hedge to the apple tree, I looked uphill, toward the bus stop on Tappan Avenue. I rubbed my eyes to clear the salty tears, and my sisters Sarah, Margie, and Vicky finally burst into view, running toward me with their cat-eye glasses and pigtails streaming behind them.

"What happened? What does it mean?" I cried, but my sisters flew past me, ignoring my pleas.

I followed them into the house and watched as they dumped their book bags willy-nilly onto the landing. Then they ran into the kitchen, grabbing their cookies and milk and plunking themselves down at the dining room table, which was nothing more than a plain old door with legs screwed onto the corners, and a hole where the doorknob used to be.

Maybe it was just another day for my sisters, but the moment I saw Ginya holding her head in her hands in the kitchen, my understanding of the world

I CALLED HER GINYA

Catherine Braik-Selin

changed. Ginya cried real tears just like me. My mother never cried. She just got angry.

Before Ginya moved in, I'd try to get my mother's attention, but she'd snap at me with "Not now, I'm busy!" or "Get out of the kitchen!" She was tall and angular, thin-lipped, and wore her hair pulled back in a prim bun. By day, she worked as a computer programmer and systems analyst, helping to land the first man on the moon. By night, with her jug of Gallo sherry and a lipstick-stained cigarette dangling from her lip, her words slurring together, she'd say, "Girls! Set the table and stop making all that noise!" After we set the table, we often waited hours for dinner as she became increasingly incapacitated.

We'd cry, "Mama, we're starving! When are we going to eat?" And she'd say, "God, I have to work all day and come home to this? Leave me alone, you brats!"

Ginya, on the other hand, seemed to have all the patience in the world, and never raised her voice.

I CALLED HER GINYA

Catherine Braik-Selin

When I was upset, she lifted me up onto her lap, whether her apron was dusted in flour or not, humming and calming me down with a gentle melody. With all the tumult in our household, she taught me how to trust.

She was from South Carolina, and I later learned she'd left school in the fifth grade to pick cotton.

"Fetch that rolling pin for me, honey child," she'd say, her languorous voice sweet as summer rain. When I looked up at her and asked, "Can I roll out the dough, please?" her tawny eyes looked as warm as a cat on a sunny windowsill. She let me bake with her in the kitchen any time I wanted, and if I got hurt playing outside, she carefully placed a Band-Aid on my scraped knee and said, "Be a big girl, now. That ain't nothin' but a cat scratch. Now, go on and play!"

But I never knew, until he showed up at our door in Norwood, New Jersey, that Ginya had a son named Michael who she'd left behind in South Carolina. He was eleven when he arrived and moved

I CALLED HER GINYA

Catherine Braik-Selin

into the attic bedroom that Sarah and Margie had shared. The room I shared with Vicky was right next to his, while Ginya had the third room, which was slightly larger than a broom closet at the top of the stairs. Sarah and Margie moved into the nursery on the second floor, and poor Charlie's crib was squeezed into the TV room across the hall from the bathroom.

Not only did Michael take Ginya's attention away from me, he also caused her no end of trouble, acting out in school and at home. He was big for his age, and he scared me. I couldn't know how difficult it was for Michael to leave the Jim Crow South in 1965, only to wind up in an all-white suburban enclave. When he entered eighth grade in New Jersey, the odds were stacked against him from day one. He tested out the waters on Margie and Vicky, then ultimately settled on me as the target for his rage and frustration. Left out of all the big girl stuff my older sisters did, I was easily cornered and manipulated. He assaulted me for three years,

I CALLED HER GINYA

Catherine Braik-Selin

beginning when I was 7 until I was 10 years old. In all that time, I never told a soul, and it only came to an end when they moved.

***

In 1968, Ginya took another job in a town closer to New York City. Maybe my mother's drinking and the dysfunction in our household became unbearable to her. Most likely my parents let her go because they could no longer afford to pay her salary.

In the days leading up to their departure, I clung to Ginya fiercely, curling up on her little cot when she packed up her few belongings. There was a length of fabric that covered the bare joists serving as shelves for her things. It had a floral pattern in warm shades of orange, ivory and green that still holds a place in the patchwork quilt of my memory.

When she sorted through her jewelry box and pulled out a necklace, I remember saying something like, "Oh, that's a pretty necklace, Ginya!"

"Well, it's my favorite – it was my mama's before me," she explained.

I CALLED HER GINYA

Catherine Braik-Selin

I think I asked her where her mama was.

"Oh, she's long gone." As detached from my own mother as I already was, I envied the longing that made Ginya's voice tremble a little bit when she talked about her own mother.

"I'm gonna miss you so much, Ginya" I cried, and wrapped my arms around her waist.

"I'm sure going miss you too, Cathy!" she said, stroking my hair. "But you're going be all right, 'cuz you're a very clever, strong girl."

The day she and Michael moved away, I sulked and tried to reconcile the loss of my savior with the release from my tormentor. From the attic window, under the eaves, I watched them lug their suitcases down the walk and through the hedge towards the waiting car. Ginya's love was now part of me, and something I could choose to hold onto. The gall of shame that festered within me was something I now had the power to destroy, and I *did* feel clever and strong at that moment. I was ready to throw away the key to my imagined hideaway.

I CALLED HER GINYA

Catherine Braik-Selin

As Ginya opened the car's passenger door, she paused. With a look on her face as though she'd forgotten something, she looked left, then right, then up towards my little tear-stained face in the attic window. Her face broke into a smile and she waved.

I opened the window and yelled, "Bye, bye, Ginya! I love you!" I could see Michael skulking in the back seat and didn't fully believe my nightmare was over.

"I hate you, Michael!" I hissed, under my breath, glaring at him through the torn window screen, until all I could see were the car's taillights at the top of the hill.

I pocketed my Tony the Tiger flashlight and a pair of scissors and retreated into the little closet that my sisters and I had made into a secret playhouse. Over and over, I scratched "I hate you, Michael" into the chalky, old drywall, gouging a hole right through it, and cut my finger. Drops of my blood splattered the pink strip of newly exposed insulation. I couldn't run to Ginya anymore for a Band-Aid, but I didn't

I CALLED HER GINYA

Catherine Braik-Selin

need her now. I wrapped my finger in an old sock and wore the pain like a badge of courage.

Until I wrote this story, it never occurred to me that Ginya may have left because she found out what was going on with Michael. The thought of her leaving to protect and not abandon me gives me great comfort 50 years later. Her love sustained me through the pain; it was the ballast that enabled me to navigate the trauma of my childhood and create a different life for my own children, a life where they never doubted they were safe and loved.

NELLIE BLY & ME

Kate Braithwaite

I'd been living with Nellie Bly in my head for some years before the accident. She was bold and ground-breaking: a young woman determined to be a successful journalist, who checked herself into an asylum, posed as a lunatic, and reported on conditions from the inside in order to secure a coveted job at Joseph Pulitzer's *New York World* newspaper. Her character, and her lack of emotion as a journalist, intrigued me. By September 2018, she was my full-time preoccupation. I signed a contract to complete a novel about her by Christmas.

Two days later my son Max had an accident. I say 'accident,' but my family has used other terms for it in the years since it happened. We started with 'near drowning' or sometimes just 'drowning' because that's what he was doing, in the shallow end of the YMCA pool, until Nathan, his teammate, noticed Max hadn't come up after the flip-turn. While everyone else was back at the deep end, Max was nowhere to be seen. I've imagined it often. The

Kate Braithwaite

shifting surface of the water, the wash of realization in Nathan's mind. A shout perhaps. Panic. The slap of bodies charging through water. The spray. Max was already over six feet tall back then, long-limbed, beluga-like. It took four people to pull him out and land him on the deck, and as I imagine it, his unconscious 15-year-old body was heavy in their hands, limp and unresponsive.

While it happened, I was walking with a friend in Longwood Gardens. My phone rang. It was Max's older brother.

"Max has just nearly died at the Y. He's unconscious. In an ambulance. Dad and I are coming to get you now."

We drove to Nemours Hospital unsure if he was alive or dead. We needed him, willed him, to still be alive. By the time we found him in Accident and Emergency, he was sitting up and fully conscious.

"What happened?" I asked, laughing through tears, cupping his face in my hands.

NELLIE BLY & ME

Kate Braithwaite

"I think I just blacked out," he said. "I woke up in the ambulance. I couldn't remember who the president was."

Even in that early explosion of relief, the questions began. Healthy 15-year-olds who have been swimming on a team since they were eight are not supposed to just drown. Doctors don't like it, I've found. They quickly ruled out drugs, but suspected heart problems. Max was admitted to the cardio unit, and specialists looked for explanations. After a battery of heart tests failed to provide answers, a neurological exam showed erratic brain waves, consistent with Juvenile Myoclonic Epilepsy. Max looked bemused, and I wept in the bathroom. Since the earliest hours in the hospital he'd insisted he was perfectly healthy and should be allowed to go home, but when it came to the details of what had happened, he was fuzzy and confused. He'd "felt weird" in the water. He'd "gone in and out." Now he was "fine" and wanted to know when he could swim again. The answer was anti-seizure medication.

NELLIE BLY & ME

Kate Braithwaite

"So, I can't swim unless I take the pills?" he asked the doctor.

"Absolutely not. You can't be in the water alone. You can't swim for two months while you adjust to the Depakote." She was blunt. It wasn't up for debate. Max began taking pills and a few days later we went home.

A semblance of normal life resumed. The shock to the family was significant and yet hard to quantify. Max spoke of the funeral he might have had: "I hope you'd have had me cremated, not buried," he said. "Would Granddad have been well enough to fly over for it?"

He revelled in the 'what-ifs': "Would swim team even have continued if…" "How sad would you have been if…"

I felt a lingering anxiety, like that itch to glance over your shoulder as you walk alone down a dark street. Every day we carried on as normal, but in my mind I was stuck, perpetually swaying on the balls of my feet, caught in that moment of stepping back from

NELLIE BLY & ME

Kate Braithwaite

the precipice, where I'd looked into the void that is the loss of a child. There was a constant sense of danger, as if I'd torn the tissue-like fabric between happiness and disaster. Every day we stood on fragile ground, braced for another seizure. I returned to that time in the early days of motherhood when I crept into their rooms looking for the rise and fall of their chests, listening for the whistle of a breath through their baby lips. I watched Max for signs of twitching, or absence. I filled out forms, took medication to the nurse, and applied for a 504 educational plan to accommodate his newly diagnosed disability. If he needed to miss more school, they would offer him extra time to complete assignments. He'd have access to water and snacks when he took his SATs. I reassured relatives in the U.K., booked blood tests and further EEG's at the hospital, and returned to Nellie Bly.

I had seventy thousand or so more words to write by the end of the year. It was demanding but the work kept me sane. I decided to give her two timelines –

NELLIE BLY & ME

Kate Braithwaite

one for her asylum experience and the other much later, in the last years of her life. In her fifties, Nellie lived in the Hotel McAlpin, just across from Macy's, and from it, she ran an informal adoption agency and wrote opinion pieces for the *New York Evening Journal*. I told the later story from the point of view of her young secretary, Beatrice, an ordinary person — a stand in for myself in effect — who found herself in the orbit of someone really quite extraordinary and was determined to puzzle her out. I read Nellie's "Ten Days in a Mad-House" over and over, exasperated by her lack of emotion. She was only 23 years old in 1887 and must have been desperately afraid during her time in the asylum. I wanted to explore that fear.

In the months that followed the accident, I invested in Nellie's story and her emotions, while our family drama simmered in the background. Christmas came and went. Somehow, I delivered my manuscript on time and began work on the edits. In hindsight, I see that I chose Nellie's feelings instead

NELLIE BLY & ME

Kate Braithwaite

of my own. I wrote a scene where Tilly Mayard, a girl Nellie befriended in the asylum, had a seizure, without thinking about Max's experience at all. I didn't link our stay in a hospital ward — our waxing lyrical about the food, or our feelings about the doctors and the tests and the treatments — to the story I was writing, even though the parallels were everywhere. I focused instead on Nellie's independence of thought, a trait I admired more and more. She was strong, instinctive, and not afraid to follow those instincts, however risky the path.

"Mom," Max said, one day at breakfast. "You know that voice inside your head, when you talk to yourself about stuff?"

"Yup. Internal monologue. Dad always says he doesn't have one." I rolled my eyes. We've never believed him about this.

"Well, I've lost mine," said Max. "I miss it."

Other changes were more obvious. He gained weight. His grades tanked. He got up, took his pills, went to school, swam, took his pills, and went to bed.

NELLIE BLY & ME

Kate Braithwaite

On the weekends, he took the pills, went swimming, came home, and slept all afternoon. There were no traumas, no twitches, no seizures. But there was also no Max. I started keeping a diary of his sleep patterns. We looked more closely at the side-effects of his anti-seizure med, Depakote. Then, my husband said starkly one day, "I want my son back."

"I know," I said. "Me too."

Nellie Bly did not have children. But she did find homes for abandoned or orphaned boys and girls. And when one of those boys lay sick and neglected in Bellevue, she didn't hesitate to have him moved to a better hospital. She didn't wait for permission from doctors or the New York Society for the Prevention of Cruelty to Children, who were legally responsible for the boy. Nellie Bly took action, and I recognized this in her, not just in the parts of her life that I chose to write about, but throughout. Sometimes she was right and sometimes she wasn't. But she was decisive and she knew when to be bold.

NELLIE BLY & ME

Kate Braithwaite

When a blood test prompted the doctors to suggest we increase Max's medication, we didn't do it. We reduced it instead. We pushed back. We were bold. Max and I went to our primary care physician and rattled off a list of the side effects he was suffering. We asked her to support us in stopping the pills and requested Nemours Hospital run new tests. She agreed.

Max was fully weaned off the medication by March, 2019. We returned to the hospital for an EEG and waited to hear the result. A neurologist called me. Not the one we had seen when Max was first admitted.

"The scan was completely normal," he said. "It's like this: five years ago, he would never have been diagnosed. We didn't make the diagnosis after only one event. But so many cases of Juvenile Myoclonic Epilepsy were missed that we changed the guidelines. Max can stay off the meds. He's fine."

Max has been medication and seizure-free ever since. He still swims and will swim in college after

Kate Braithwaite

he graduates high school this year. I'm so thankful for his resilience and for Nellie Bly who, in those months, quietly taught me that it was okay to trust my instinct. Her example showed me that we are stronger than we know, and I'm forever inspired by her maxim that "energy applied rightly and directed will accomplish anything." I respect her belief in her instincts and her courage to go her own way. I needed that to push back against Max's diagnosis. He would have spent years, possibly decades, dulled by Depakote, if we had complied with the doctors. But taking another leaf out of Nellie Bly's book, we've never spent time getting emotional about it all. Max might have been angry about what he went through, but instead, he chose to move on.

"I'll write about it for my college essay, Mom," he said, last spring. "You know, about that thing that happened. But then I'm done with it. It's done."

WHERE THERE'S A WILL

Marlén Cordova-Pedroza

"Where there's a will, there's a way," my mentor Ms. Perna said. It was the first time I'd heard the phrase in English. She was giving a talk during the Walk In Knowledge program that she directs at Kennett High School, encouraging students to follow their dreams, even if it seems impossible. I was a freshman then. Now I'm a senior, and I reflect on her words when I'm feeling down about my senior year. I never envisioned life during a pandemic, or 'online school,' or missing out on fun teenage events like pep rallies, prom, homecoming, and football games.

I was just a little girl when I met Ms. Perna. The day she arrived at my house, my older sisters and brothers sat patiently on the big, red sofa in our apartment, waiting for her. My mother brushed my untamable black hair, and I asked her, "Porque me tengo que ver bien, quien viene?" *Why do I have to dress up? Who's coming?*

"Es una mujer que no conoces de la escuela de tus hermanos para hablar con tu papa." *She's a*

WHERE THERE'S A WILL

Marlén Cordova-Pedroza

*woman you don't know, from your siblings' school,
to speak with your dad.*

I wanted to know why.

"Para hablar del colegio." *To talk about college.*

At six, I didn't know what "college" meant, but I knew it must be important, because the whole family had to be there to hear about it. We only gathered like this for Christmas or to attend church.

When Ms. Perna arrived, I stared at her long, black hair. She carried lots of papers and wore a blouse and high heels. Her bright, white smile and silky hair reminded me of the Disney princesses on TV.

My eldest sister, Janet, wanted to go to this place called "college," but my father didn't like the idea. He was afraid he'd lose control over her; he controlled almost everything she did. He constantly told her, "Quiero que empieces a trabajar." *I want you to start working.* But Janet wanted something different.

My father thought she was abandoning the family by pursuing her own education. He grew up in a

WHERE THERE'S A WILL

Marlén Cordova-Pedroza

household that prioritized work over school, and he'd didn't know anyone who attended college. It seemed like a fantasy to him, too good to be true, and certainly not realistic.

When my sister Beatriz, the second oldest, heard that my father wouldn't let Janet go to college, she got involved. She knew Ms. Perna from middle school and confided in her. Later that week, Beatriz said, "Va a venir una mujer de la escuela para hablar contigo del colegio hoy." *A woman from my school will be coming to talk to you about college today.* My dad looked at my mom, and she nodded, adding, "Asegurate de estar aquí cuando llegue." *Make sure you're here when she arrives.*

Ms. Perna brought lots of brochures with her that day about how to apply to college. She explained that my parents didn't have to worry about not being able to afford it. Janet could apply for financial aid and scholarships. My mom asked questions here and there during the meeting, but when I got older, I learned that she didn't know what kind of questions to ask Ms. Perna; she never finished school and

WHERE THERE'S A WILL

Marlén Cordova-Pedroza

began working when she was very young. My father sat silently, but when Ms. Perna told him that she understood his biggest fear was letting Janet leave, his face became more relaxed. She went on to explain that sooner or later Janet would leave his side. He could watch her rebel against him or allow her to go. My father hesitated, but finally gave his blessing, then said, "Ahora es tu responsabilidad." *She is now your responsibility.*

Janet's face lit up like a light bulb, she smiled so much; I'd never seen her so happy. Finally, both of my parents had given her their permission. She told me later that she didn't want to let them down or Ms. Perna. As the oldest, she did feel pressure, but she was also excited for my family, knowing that if she could successfully graduate college, the rest of us might be able to attend.

That day, Ms. Perna opened the door to opportunity and growth for all of us.

***

I too dreamed of going to college, but at the beginning of high school, things were not going well.

WHERE THERE'S A WILL

Marlén Cordova-Pedroza

I was struggling. Before ninth grade, I wasn't given the opportunity to choose the classes I wanted; in middle school, the teachers made those decisions for me. And when I asked for higher level classes, the teachers said things like, "You're doing just fine in this class, so why would you want to take a class where you'll end up with Cs or Ds?"

I was frustrated in middle school that no one saw the potential in me that I saw in myself. I knew I was capable of more; I just needed someone to give me the chance to prove it. So when high school arrived, I finally chose what *I* wanted: four honors courses, my freshman year.

I went to see Ms. Perna almost daily, and sometimes, I entered her office crying. Ms. Perna stopped what she was doing and listened to me. My honors science class was giving me the most trouble. Compared to my classmates, I was getting really low scores, even after I'd spent hours and hours studying, and lunch periods reviewing the work with my teacher. I sat in Ms. Perna's black swivel chair and spun around and around, unsure of what to do.

WHERE THERE'S A WILL

Marlén Cordova-Pedroza

"Marlén, what's wrong?" she asked.

Unable to hold them back any longer, I let my tears fall. "I think I need to drop my science class," I said.

I described how defeated I felt hearing other students brag about not studying and still achieving perfect scores. But there was *more*. I told Ms. Perna I felt different -- 'different' because of my brown skin color, my dark eyes, and my black hair. I was the only Latina in my honors classes, and I wasn't able to connect with the other students; we lived such different lifestyles. While many of my peers would spend their summers traveling, I spent mine working, cleaning, and cooking at home. I was scared to talk, or give my opinion in class, for fear that the white kids would think I was stupid. Around them, I didn't feel "smart enough."

Ms. Perna handed me tissues to wipe my tears and reminded me, "Marlén, you are intelligent, and you belong in those classes. You *deserve* to be there. I will not let you think less of yourself."

WHERE THERE'S A WILL

Marlén Cordova-Pedroza

After that, I couldn't bring myself to drop the class, though I thought it would solve my problems. Ms. Perna suggested and arranged a tutor for me, and we met every Monday and Thursday. Oftentimes, when I was not understanding a concept, my tutor Lauren made flashcards or Quizlets for me to review. I soon found this study method worked best for me.

Lauren also taught me how to do basic outlines and new ways to interact with the text, other than just taking notes. When we first met, she said, "Marlén, one B- is not bad at all! Maybe it wasn't the grade you expected, but you should feel good about how hard you've worked."

At the end of ninth grade, I was immensely proud of the 'B' I earned in that class, because I earned it with my own sweat and tears. And even though I worked ten times harder than other students to understand the material, I still succeeded, and I learned that a test grade doesn't define me; it's the effort I put in that truly matters.

Without Ms. Perna's help and encouragement during my freshman year of high school, I would

WHERE THERE'S A WILL

Marlén Cordova-Pedroza

have switched to a regular class and taken the easy way out. Now, as I apply to colleges and ask myself *How will you pay for school? How many loans will you need? How will you pay them back if you don't get a good job?* it's still Ms. Perna's reassuring voice I hear: "Nothing rewarding is ever easy, Marlén."

My family and I are grateful for Ms. Perna's guidance through the years. She provided me with opportunities that helped me to grow into a more confident person. Without her mentorship, I wouldn't be the person I am now – my siblings wouldn't either. My father now regrets being so strict with my sister Janet twelve years ago. Today, he cannot imagine a life where all five of his children *didn't* attend college

Frida Kahlo once said, "Soy del tipo de mujer que si quiero la luna, me la bajo yo solita!" *I'm the type of woman that if I want the moon, I'll get it all by myself!* Her words remind me of "where there's a will, there's a way," because I know that when I work hard I'm able to achieve my goals. I saw this come true in my high school classes when I achieved

WHERE THERE'S A WILL

Marlén Cordova-Pedroza

higher grades, which encouraged me to want a college degree.

I also want to attend law school after college. My dad is a farmworker who works twelve-hour shifts, or more, every day. He works in a dark and damp environment with his back perpetually bent in half, cutting mushrooms for minimum wage. His experience as a 'picker' has influenced how I plan to use my education: to get a law degree and fight for improved working conditions for farmworkers. Most importantly, I see myself in the future speaking to the workers in mushroom houses and letting them know they're not alone in their battle. I will fight with them, just as I've fought hard to earn my education.

I'll always be inspired by the words of my mentor, Loretta Perna, and Frida Kahlo, two women I greatly admire and respect, who've taught me to dream big and never forget that I have the power within me to achieve what I want. I'm an intelligent, courageous, powerful, and beautiful Latina, ready to face the world and all its challenges.

DREAMS OF MY MOTHER

Eve Rachel Fisher

It's almost 2020. I have a lump in my breast that will soon be biopsied. I dread the feeling of helplessness that will accompany being laid out on a table with my body vulnerable, my breast exposed. I know the panic I'll feel, wondering what is being made visible beneath my skin. I remember the fear that rose in me following the initial ultrasound. After the doctor left the room, I lay on the table and watched the clock, counting sixty seconds, 30 times, to keep my mind from running wild. When she returned with a second doctor, I knew it wasn't good. I started crying when they told me that they had found something suspicious and that I would need to have a biopsy. But I try not to think of the procedure that awaits me. Instead, I think of my mother.

One more year has passed without her. Some mornings, when I'm feeling particularly distraught, I pull her old black flannel robe from my closet, wrap myself up in it, and try to remember her giving me a hug. The robe smells more like me now than what I used to call her "mother smell." We laughed about it,

DREAMS OF MY MOTHER

Eve Rachel Fisher

because she never used anything particularly perfumy. We joked that it was something primal, and I guess it was, because my brain still conjures her scent, and I can still feel the way her body enveloped mine in a hug, even though she was shorter and thinner than I am. I think of the little line she had above her lip from smiling. She hated the few wrinkles she had, but that line was endearing to me. Even when she wasn't smiling, it reminded me of the love that radiated from her to me through her smile.

Sometimes I feel she sends me a sign. I know how unlikely this is. I know this is something the bereaved invoke to convince themselves they're still connected to the dead.

As I near my parents' house to visit my father, I spot a flourishing plant at the base of the steps leading to the front door, growing in the space where the corner of the brick meets the sidewalk. This is not so magical; weeds push up everywhere. But this is a Jewels of Opar, a plant I've only seen at the botanical garden where I used to work. Its dense, pale-green leaves release into long, delicate fronds, with

DREAMS OF MY MOTHER

Eve Rachel Fisher

miniscule pink, star-shaped flowers opening only at dusk. The flowers mature into perfectly round, red-and-gold seedpods. My mother loved this plant. I collected a bag of seeds for her, but she got sick before she could put them in the ground. I walk up and down the street, looking for a reasonable explanation: *the seeds must have spread from another plant.* But there are no others.

Before first frost, I cut off a stalk and put it in water. As the new year approaches, the plant sits rooted in soil, flowering in the sun on the round white kitchen table where my mother fed me so many meals. In my last memory of her at this table, she exclaimed, "This is glorious!" as she devoured a ripe mango I had cut up for her.

Another day, missing her terribly and at loose ends, I wander over to my bookshelf and open one of the antique tins she collected. I discover a rose quartz arrowhead accompanied by a small note in her neat, rounded handwriting: "*I found this in the field next to our friend Joann's house in the '70s. I was thrilled. - A.F.*" I feel elation at her words, her handwriting, her

DREAMS OF MY MOTHER

Eve Rachel Fisher

initials. *Anne Fisher*. It's a gift to know the warm hands I so loved had carefully folded the tissue around the arrowhead, anticipating as she wrote the note that I, or my brother or father, would one day find it.

On a rare night alone in the house, I find myself sitting on the floor of my bedroom with a box of my mother's things. There is one of her ubiquitous silky nightgowns, her slippers, a book of crosswords with her answers written in pen. And there are the hats, wrapped carefully in white tissue paper, that I suddenly realize she must have knitted for the children I will never have. There are two baby-size hats with pompoms, a larger hat that would fit a toddler, and one for an older child. She must have thought I would have a boy because they're all shades of blue and brown. There's also a delicate navy-blue blanket, just the right size for a crib.

When my mother was dying and no longer speaking, I whispered in her ear, "Come visit me, okay?" The first dream came eight days after her death, and then so frequently that I often woke up

DREAMS OF MY MOTHER

Eve Rachel Fisher

exhausted, drained by the emotion I experienced in my sleep. The dreams were either distressing (I'm frantically trying to call her but the phone won't work, and I know she's about to die), or gratifying (elevator doors open to reveal her, and I drop everything I'm carrying to engulf her in my arms).

She's mostly silent in these dreams, appearing sometimes to be an image of my own making, and devoted solely to my well-being: she holds up a pair of my shoes with worn-down heels, as if to tell me to replace them, or opens the refrigerator to reveal an enormous chicken she's cooked for me, or takes away my old, holey socks and replaces them with her own intact ones.

Then come the dreams, in the later years following her death, where she is seemingly her own brave and independent person. She runs down the sidewalk barefoot in winter. She nestles birds in the crook of her elbow. She carries a kayak on her shoulder up flights of stairs. She picks up dead mice. My reaction in these dreams is part incredulity, part admiration, part consternation. I try to slow her

DREAMS OF MY MOTHER

Eve Rachel Fisher

down. I call after her. I tell her to be careful. But she continues on, unheeding of me.

Now, after eight years, she hardly ever appears. I'm frustrated by this; I somehow need her more the longer she is gone. This seems counterintuitive: shouldn't I need her less now, having integrated my mother more fully into my sense of self? Shouldn't other relationships have filled the void of her loss? Shouldn't I be more evolved? I can't help feeling that I did it wrong somehow, "it" being this process of mourning.

My life would be unrecognizable to her now. When she died in 2012, I was thirty-nine, single, living in San Francisco, and working as a nanny. She doesn't know that I moved back to the East Coast, that I got married, that I'm now considering divorce. She doesn't know I became a stepmother, or that I went through numerous rounds of IVF in a failed attempt to have a child.

My mother would be unhappy that I married someone with so much baggage – two kids, a contentious divorce, an ex-wife he still battles. She

DREAMS OF MY MOTHER

Eve Rachel Fisher

would be sad that I have tethered myself to someone who suffers from depression and anxiety. She would be baffled that I married a man who had a vasectomy, when all I wanted my entire life was to be a mother.

She would approve of me exercising regularly, but she'd worry that I am getting too thin, and upon hearing about one of my busy days, would say, "You must be exhausted."

She'd be proud of me for getting my writing published. An aunt told me that my mother had taken a long time to choose my name; because I would be an adult longer than I'd be a child, she wanted me to have a grown-up name. She had also said that I might decide to become an author, and that "Eve Rachel Fisher" would be fitting.

My mother would be horrified by the way my father regales me with his sexual escapades. She wouldn't be surprised that he began dating within six months of her death, though; she predicted that.

I don't know what she'd make of my living at a Zen Buddhist monastery for a year after her death, waking at 4:30am and meditating for two hours every

DREAMS OF MY MOTHER

Eve Rachel Fisher

morning. She'd probably think it was a cult. I often imagined her watching me do all that chanting and bowing; I had to admit that it did feel a bit cult-like.

My mother would think it ridiculous that we kept all her clothes, that her drawers are stuffed with her knitting needles and yarn. She would have been much more practical about getting rid of her possessions.

I don't think she'd be thrilled that my father shares his medical marijuana with me.

She'd be happy that I've become close to her friend Diane, though I always feel a twinge of sadness when I meet her for lunch, wishing it was my mother I was on my way to see. People often assume we are mother and daughter, which infuriates me. The little girl in me wants to snarl at these people, "She's *not* my mom!"

The one thing I can't fathom is my mother knowing about my brother's death. Her firstborn, her only son, died a year after she did. I simultaneously thank God that she wasn't alive to see it, and believe wholeheartedly that had she been alive, his death

DREAMS OF MY MOTHER

Eve Rachel Fisher

could not have happened. I can't imagine a world in which my mother would have allowed my brother to die.

The biopsy is now imminent, and I can't avoid the thought of it any longer. I try to think of what my mother would say to comfort me, but I can't find her words. I remember instead all that she endured, much worse than my mere biopsy, during her treatment for cancer: surgery, chemotherapy, radiation, spinal taps, and her body's final failure, with all its attendant humiliations.

As I lie on the table for the procedure, with my right arm above my head, after the doctor has injected the lidocaine into my breast and started using ultrasound to locate the lump, I will close my eyes and see my mother. I won't imagine her as I last saw her, her eyes closed and her cheekbones prominent, beautiful even in her unresponsiveness. I remember instead the look on her face when I caught her watching me doing absolutely nothing – clearing the table, eating a sandwich, trying to come up with a word during one of our Scrabble games. I would

DREAMS OF MY MOTHER

Eve Rachel Fisher

ask, "What?" and she would say "Nothing," but her adoration shone like the glow of sunlight from the grin on her face. I basked in that warmth her whole life. It was as though my mere existence thrilled her. I never saw that look on anyone's face but hers.

That's what I'll concentrate on, waiting for the lump to be located, the needle inserted, the cells biopsied. I'll see my mother, loving me.

THE WILD CAT

Erica Mier

Snowflakes whirled and drifted around my head before falling to the ground. I tilted my head backwards and stuck out my tongue to taste the soft crystals. Magic wandered over to me, her black and gold tail whipping back and forth, and she began to purr. My father stood several feet away, talking to our neighbor about grownup stuff. I didn't hear what they said, because Magic was making figure eights between my legs. I called her "my" cat, but Magic belonged to the mountain. I named her Magic because she sometimes disappeared for days, then reappeared out of nowhere.

Mom. My heart ached to think of her. She and my little brother Jeb were four hours away and living in Pennsylvania. Her laughter and singing, our dancing, the sweet scent of grapes that we picked together, bubbling on the stove, becoming jam, no longer filled our home. Instead, her ghost haunted the house.

My father was awarded temporary custody of me because the judge didn't want to remove me from my home or school in Virginia, in case my mother

THE WILD CAT

Erica Mier

returned. Biting my lip to fight the tears, I took off my winter glove and scratched behind Magic's velvety ears. The familiar motor of her purr comforted me. She sank her claws deep into the padding of my pink snowsuit and climbed toward my arms. I continued petting her soft fur, remembering a warm day in Mom's flower garden when Magic and I trailed after her musical voice.

"Get that damn cat off you!" my father spat, smacking Magic off me. She took off running. Wild as she was, I knew she'd be back. She loved me.

"She wrecked your snowsuit," he said, glaring at me, and cold silence filled the space between us. I counted the days until I could see Mom and Jeb again.

My parents' marriage of twenty years had just ended. My father's infidelities weren't the reason; Mom left because he demanded five-year-old Jeb be institutionalized. Shortly after my brother was born, he was diagnosed with severe, profound mental retardation and cerebral palsy. He never learned to walk or speak, or to bathe or dress himself. He ate

THE WILD CAT

Erica Mier

with his hands, crawled, and made loud noises to communicate pleasure or disapproval.

When Mom refused to send him away, my father threatened to leave. She decided to leave him instead, and took Jeb and me to live with my grandmother. My father sought custody of me and initially won. But once Mom finalized the divorce, she was awarded primary custody of us both. In a rage, my father demanded that I stop speaking to her. He encouraged me to run away, threatened to kidnap me, and detailed his plans of suicide if I didn't help him. I dreaded his visitation days.

"I suppose your letters just got 'lost' in the mail again?" he said. Cigarette smoke swirled around his face, permeating the car; the fumes burned the back of my throat. I stifled the urge to cough. Coughing would only make him angrier.

"I think so," I said. "I mean, I know I mailed *some.*" I said, clutching the plastic Bart Simpson doll from the Burger King kids' meal. I rubbed my fingers over Bart's bulging eyes and felt my stomach tighten into painful knots. I couldn't eat.

THE WILD CAT

Erica Mier

"The deal was you are to write to me every single day," he said. He'd told me to write down how much I wanted to be with him, and how much I hated my mother.

"I know, Dad. I am," I said, looking down.

"That damn mailman. I knew he was in cahoots with your grandmother."

The knots in my stomach tightened. I feared that our mailman would get into trouble because of my lie about the letters. I'd sworn to my father that I'd put them in my grandmother's mailbox.

The scent of his cinnamon Dentyne gum drifted into the hazy smoke. He chewed angrily.

"What about the judge? Did you remember to write to him this week? Or could you not be bothered?"

"Dad, I did," I said.

"Listen, if you don't want to fight to be together, you can just live with that mother of yours. If you don't love me, I'm going to quit fighting."

"No, Daddy. I'm still fighting. I love you."

THE WILD CAT

Erica Mier

"Well, if you don't want to be with me, I just can't be on this earth."

My sweaty hands trembled. My father gave me vivid descriptions of his plans for suicide, one of which entailed driving his car off a cliff at Sky Line Drive, near the house we once shared in the mountains. I imagined his car careening off one of the edges while happy families posed for pictures at the scenic vista.

In the two years that followed my parents' divorce, my father remarried and divorced a second time. He struggled to keep a steady job and was forced to sell our mountain home in Virginia. He moved into the guest bedroom of his parents' house in New Jersey, and all of my visitations with him took place there. As a ten-year-old, I'd creep to the bathroom in that house, lock the door, and chug Pepto Bismol to relieve the pain in my stomach. Then I lay in bed picturing myself telling him I didn't want to be with him anymore. But when I saw his sad eyes again, I couldn't bring myself to do it.

THE WILD CAT

Erica Mier

The last time I saw him was the weekend of my eleventh birthday. His family tried to make it special. There was cake. There were presents. We spent the day with his parents, his sister, and my cousins, picnicking and swimming at a lake in South Jersey. It was easier to be with him when other people were there to deflect his attention. I decided I would tell him I didn't want to be with him anymore during the last moments of our visitation. But then, standing on my mother's front porch about to say goodbye, I stared at his brown eyes and watched them turn red from crying, and again, I couldn't do it.

"I love you, Pumpkin," he said. "I'm going to miss you."

"I'm going to miss you, too," I said, my throat tightening. It wasn't a lie, but it wasn't the truth, either. I loved him, but he was more than I knew how to handle. I hugged him and felt the pain return to my stomach.

"I'll call you tonight, Pumpkin." He squeezed me one last time, kissed my cheek, and walked down the steps. I watched him get into his car and buckle his

THE WILD CAT

Erica Mier

seat belt. He lit a cigarette. I smiled and waved at him before going inside. But I didn't want him to call me later – I wanted to be done.

Later that week, I took the easy way out and told him on the phone that I couldn't "fight" to be with him anymore. To my relief, no suicide resulted, but he quickly disappeared from our lives. Not long after, Margaret arrived.

***

"Margaret" was too formal. We called her Maggie. She was in her early twenties with curly, golden hair that air-dried to perfection. She never needed braces, like I did. She worked at Jeb's school, and watched him afterward so Mom could do chores and go food shopping without having to push his wheelchair beside her cart.

Since I was little, Mom had a chronic autoimmune disease: scleroderma. Her flare-ups were worse during the winter, but they also came on during times of stress. Her fingers would swell and turn hot and bright red. Sometimes, they turned white because blood couldn't get to them. When it was

THE WILD CAT

Erica Mier

cold, she was always in more pain, her white fingers
turning dark purple with open, oozing sores. Later, I
found out the condition moved to her toes and
elbows. Since Mom worked full time as a nurse,
Maggie lifted some of her burden, and mine too. She
meshed so well with our family that she soon took on
more hours. I was too old for a babysitter by age
twelve, but Mom liked the idea of Maggie watching
Jeb, knowing an 'extra set of eyes' would also be on
me. I never minded, because after Mom got home
from work, Maggie hung out, often staying for
dinner, and we laughed a lot. In the summer, when
Mom had to leave for work early, Maggie arrived the
night before with her overnight bag. In the morning,
she'd take Jeb and me to the pool near our house, or
to the beach.

Even a drive to the store was exciting and fun
with Maggie. She blasted country music and sang
along terribly, dancing behind the steering wheel.
During my boy-crazed middle school days, I was
entranced by her stories of various boyfriends: the
motorcycle riders, the blues band members, the

THE WILD CAT

Erica Mier

outdoors enthusiasts, the surfers. Once, after complaining about the nonexistence of my breasts, Maggie looked down at her own small chest and smirked, saying, "Well, I never had any complaints." And just like that, my AAs weren't such a liability.

She even made loving Jeb easier. I stopped feeling embarrassed when his diaper smelled or when drool dangled from his mouth, soaking his shirt. If he made loud screeching noises in a crowded public place, Maggie glanced around, found the nearest person who was staring, put on her magnetic smile, and said, "Well, I guess Jeb just wants to make sure we said hello, so... hello!"

Strangers, relieved that the awkward moment was over, seemed to also fall for Maggie. "Hello, Jeb," they'd say, smiling. If not for Maggie's warmth, my reaction would have been to give these strangers an icy death stare 'til they cowered, but nine times out of ten, Maggie made new friends.

She also helped to bridge the gap between Mom and me, the one my father had so strategically created. When my mom found herself in the throes

THE WILD CAT

Erica Mier

of menopause, and I was still struggling with puberty, it was Maggie who brought us closer.

"Woo-wee!" Mom bellowed. "I'm having my own personal summer over here!" She fanned herself dramatically as sweat beaded on her upper lip and forehead. Jeb sat unfazed at the kitchen counter, blowing loud bubbles into his cup of milk.

"Mom!" I hissed. "The entire neighborhood doesn't need to hear that you're having a hot flash." I wished I could crawl under the counter. Out of the corner of my eye, I watched Maggie. She ignored my embarrassment. Then she grabbed a piece of mail off the counter and wildly fanned my mom.

"No 'personal summers' allowed here, Elaine!" Laughing, she grabbed more mail, forcing it into Jeb's hands, saying, "Quick, Jebbers! This aging lady needs our help!"

She pulled Jeb off his stool and grasped his arms, flailing them at Mom. Jeb had no idea what was happening, but loved the commotion and attention, and started to laugh.

THE WILD CAT

Erica Mier

"Help! This is serious, Jeb!" Maggie yelled. His laughter – one of the best sounds in the world – made me smile too. Maggie noticed, grabbed more mail, and handed it to me.

"Come on, Erica! And don't worry, Elaine; it's under control! Let us know when you need us to start feeding you grapes!"

The laughter that filled our kitchen in those days was unfamiliar, but immediately, it belonged.

My teen years hit, and Maggie and I referred to each other as "sisters," something neither of us had. She snuck into my bedroom when I wasn't home and used my favorite Victoria's Secret lotions. If she spent the night at our house, I quietly crept into the bathroom while she was showering and threw a cup of ice-cold water over the shower curtain, a habit that came to a halt the day Maggie flung the curtain open and dragged me, in my pajamas, under the water with her. I was overjoyed on my 14th birthday, when she gave me two silver charms: *Brat* and *Number One Sister*. I wanted to live up to each one.

THE WILD CAT

Erica Mier

When she stayed for dinner, I stealthily downed her iced tea each time she refilled her glass. If she was about to leave, I hid her keys in the freezer. One day, she made me wait too long in the car, so I dug through her glove box and found a lone tampon. I hung it on the rear-view mirror, and we drove almost the entire way home with it swinging back and forth before she noticed it.

We laughed so hard in that little two door Nissan Sentra. She tried to teach me how to drive it and took me to a back road to learn. I failed, because not only was her car a stick shift, I was petrified of getting caught. Maggie didn't understand my need to duck below the steering wheel every time the lights of an approaching car appeared.

"Erica," she said, "what's more suspicious, a young-looking driver, or *no* driver?"

There were times we didn't see Maggie for several weeks. Mom said not to take it personally. "Maggie's like a stray cat, loved by the whole neighborhood. Don't worry when she goes away. She'll be back."

THE WILD CAT

Erica Mier

And when one of us was angry at Maggie for leaving us hanging, the other said, "It's just the wild cat in her."

***

Over the next twelve years, Mom's scleroderma slowly and painfully progressed, and Maggie helped her to accept that she could no longer care for her aging son alone. She also helped to train the caregivers who eventually looked after Jeb, continually monitoring his care. And when the disease advanced to Mom's internal organs, our "wild cat" didn't run.

Then, I turned thirty and began talking about the possibility of Mom moving in with me. The following year she did. Maggie helped Mom with the move and loved coming to visit us, since it was like old times -- the three of us together again.

I was married by that time, and Mom lived with us for six years before it was time to call for hospice. Maggie visited the night before Mom made the call; she couldn't get warm. The cold had always been the

THE WILD CAT

Erica Mier

root of her flare-ups and made her blood circulation slow down.

"I need to get warm, girls. Can you help me get into a hot shower?" she asked, trembling.

Maggie and I lifted Mom's now-50-pound body into her wheelchair and rolled her into the bathroom. Silently, all three of us realized she couldn't bathe herself alone. Maggie and I helped Mom undress, and I tried not to let her see my tears. Her tiny, skeletal body shook, and we made the water as hot as possible without burning her. We placed our shoulders under Mom's arms and hoisted her onto the shower seat, all of us soaked in the process. I lathered up a shower pouf, placed it in Mom's hand, and pulled the curtain to give her some privacy. Moments later, her breathing was audible as she fought for oxygen in the steam. Pulmonary failure is one of the last stages of scleroderma.

"I can't breathe," she gasped. "I need to get out."

I wrapped her in a towel, and together Maggie and I lifted her back into the wheelchair. The next

THE WILD CAT

Erica Mier

day, Mom made the call for hospice care to come to our home.

***

Maggie was ever-present the last few months, helping us cling to laughter like a life preserver. On Mom's last birthday, I watched my oldest son, who was four at the time, sit on Maggie's lap beside the bed. Mom, Maggie, and my son were laughing uncontrollably about something as simple as a chocolate popsicle melting and dripping down my son's hand onto Maggie's lap. Mom coughed from the exertion, but her face radiated with joy.

"What do I get a dying woman on her birthday?" I asked her.

"Time, Ery. Just time with you and our family," she said.

When Mom took her first dose of morphine, she and Maggie giggled on the bed, as Mom drunkenly announced, "Wow! This is *good* stuff."

And then, soon after, the last night arrived. The night none of us slept. The night Mom couldn't get comfortable. The night we tried to quench Mom's

THE WILD CAT

Erica Mier

thirst but watched her choke on everything we gave her. The night she slipped further and further away. The night she fought for each breath. And Maggie never left.

At around 2:00 a.m., Mom tried to communicate that she needed something, but we could no longer understand her. With one burst of effort and frustration, she screeched, "Tea!" I frantically raced into her small kitchen to heat up a cup of water. A lump formed in my throat; I was fairly certain this would be the last word I would hear her speak.

Maggie followed me, and calmly said, with a half-smile, "That woman loves her tea."

She watched me add four spoonfuls of sugar, both of us knowing there was no possible way Mom could drink it. She could no longer hold the cup, so I brought it up to her lips. Immediately, she choked.

"Just a little taste, Elaine," Maggie said.

We repeated this every few minutes the entire night: Mom begging us for a drink, placing her hand urgently on her mouth until we gave her a few drips on a spongy stick the hospice nurses provided. She choked violently for several agonizing minutes, then begged again for the tea. We didn't know to give her a higher dose of morphine. *We didn't know.*

Early the next morning, a nurse arrived and administered the right dose of morphine that Mom so badly needed to remain comfortable, but it moved her into an unconscious state. Maggie spent the day with us, again, my two sons playing happily beside Mom's bed, my husband keeping them entertained.

I'd like to think that Mom stayed with us a bit longer to hear their voices and giggles.

"Ery, I think I'll get going now," Maggie said, "I need to get some rest, take a shower, feed my cat." It was 3:00 p.m. and she had been up with me all night.

"Okay, but, um… before you go, can you help me change her, one last time?" I asked and turned to look through Mom's bedside basket for supplies. My husband, Dustin, gathered up our sons and took them to the living room.

"Of course," Maggie said, walking over to Mom.

"Come on, Elaine, help us out here."

THE WILD CAT

Erica Mier

She began to slip her hand behind Mom's neck, but then she stopped, placing her hand on Mom's shoulder.

"Ery, something is different -- her breathing."

I turned back toward Mom and saw what she meant. Mom's breathing had shifted. She was no longer fighting. Maggie and I locked eyes before each of us crawled into bed, on either side of Mom. Together, we watched the rise and fall of her chest become less frequent. The wisps of air that escaped her mouth were less and less audible. Finally, the last, gentle puff left her lips.

I reached across Mom, squeezed Maggie's hand, and smiled.

"You did it, Mom," I whispered, and for just a moment, a strange joy and relief filled my body. Her suffering was finally over. For years, I begged God to let me be with her when she passed. My wish granted, I'd been given one of the greatest gifts of my life. Tears spilled down Maggie's face, as she smiled gently at me. We'd made it, carrying Mom together

THE WILD CAT

Erica Mier

and through to the end. I knew that it was the way Mom wanted it.

"I'm going to go now, Ery," Maggie said, holding her car keys.

"Your cat's going to be very hungry," I replied.

"Call me if you need anything," she said softly, and walked to the door. "I'll be back."

"I will. Thank you, Maggie, for... *being here.* I'm going to need you."

"Well, you're not getting rid of me," she said.

Maggie might come and go, but she'd be back. Maggie always came back. Wild as she was, she loved me.

RAINBOW HILL

Erica Mier

"**I**'m not dragging this on any longer than I have to, Ery," my mother said, after I'd begged her for months to get an oxygen tank. Now she wanted to know, "What do we want our 'sign' to be?" But all I could do was stare at her blankly.

She wasn't afraid to discuss her death. She spoke of it as if she were going on a trip, a vacation, her next adventure.

"Some people do pennies," she continued, pressing the button to raise the top portion of the bed that had been delivered by hospice. She could see me better now, but the effort to adjust the bed had shifted her center of gravity, causing her to fight for breath. I listened as she strained for air and fought the tears of anger that loomed inside me.

"You know," she said, "like, pennies from heaven. Some people see them on the ground and--."

"I don't want pennies," I said, cutting her off. "I'm sorry, but I don't buy that. What do pennies have to do with the person they're remembering? All

Erica Mier

of the sudden, after they die, they have a weird affinity for pennies?"

"Well, some people do birds, like cardinals."

I glared at her.

"No, that's not a good idea," she said. "You hate birds."

"I don't *hate* birds."

"Ery, you tried to hit them with your car as a teenager."

"Ma, I never actually hit one. Besides, I was only doing it a favor, teaching it a little lesson."

"The lesson being?"

The front door opened, and my husband entered the small living room where the hospice bed took up most of the space.

"Birds don't belong in the road," I said.

Realizing it was 'that conversation,' Dustin said, "Oh, good grief. This again?"

"Hey, Dustin," Mom said. "Welcome home."

"Hey, ladies, thought I'd say hello." Dustin wiped his feet on the doormat. He walked over to me,

RAINBOW HILL

Erica Mier

planted a quick kiss on my cheek, and said, "I'll see you later," then climbed the stairway that connected to the main house. After Mom's scleroderma progressed, we built an attached studio so she could live with us.

I ended the conversation with, "No, Mom, birds *cannot* be our sign, unless you want to signal that you're haunting me."

"I'll never understand you, Ery," she said. Her loving smile calmed my anger about the oxygen tank.

Our bird disagreement had lasted decades, each of us knowing the other's script.

What do you have against birds?

They poop!

You poop!

True, but I refrain from doing it on cars.

She loved to remind me of the morning in high school when I'd awakened and found my car covered in bird shit. It was as if an entire flock had intentionally dive-bombed my car. I ran inside the house screaming, "Mom!"

RAINBOW HILL

Erica Mier

She burst into laughter upon seeing my car. "That poor little birdie must have had the tummy troubles!"

"Poor little birdie?" I said, staring at my previously maroon Dodge Shadow. It looked like it had lost a game of paintball.

Mom *loved* birds. If bread went moldy, she'd use her disease-mangled hands to awkwardly tear the bread into pieces. Then she'd toss the bread into our backyard, and yell, "Come and get it, guys!"

Perhaps she's to blame for my bird disdain, because her favorite phrase to stop my bad behavior when I was a little girl was, "If you don't knock it off, Ery, I'm going to hang you from the clothesline by your toenails and let the birds pick your brain!"

But I watched her in the kitchen as she began her day. She opened the window to listen to the birds, and drank her coffee at the counter. When the weather was nice, she moved her coffee and Bible to the screened-in porch to hear their songs. It shocked me that instead of spending money on herself, she

RAINBOW HILL

Erica Mier

splurged on bird food. Feeding the birds was her luxury; it brought her peace.

I tried to think of something that brought me peace. The ocean had always calmed my soul, but I couldn't take a trip to the beach anytime I wanted to feel Mom close. Plus, I wanted it to be something out of my control. Something I could see and know it was meant for me, not just someone's lost change. It had to be something special, something sacred, something ethereal, and something that would arrive whenever I needed it.

"What about rainbows?" I said.

"Yes! Of course!" Mom answered. "You've always loved rainbows!"

I was captivated by them as a girl. They had a magical quality, appearing when conditions were just right. Even though they only lasted for a brief, enchanting while, to me, rainbows were like a scientific message from God, as if the explanation of how one is formed – "a reflection and refraction of light and matter" – had commingled with the

RAINBOW HILL

Erica Mier

mystical art and beauty of God, and, for a few moments, opened the door between heaven and earth.

In college, speeding down the highway with my roommate Kate, we drove through a small storm and saw a rainbow begin. As it grew larger and brighter, we watched it move nearer to us.

"Look, Kate!" I yelled. "It's almost perfect!"

"It's so close!" she said. "Almost end-to-end. But, wait… is the other end? Is it…"

"You're seeing this too, right?" I said, barely able to move for fear I'd break the spell.

The rainbow began across the sky on our left, and the other end was… the hood of our car!

"Kate," I asked. "Is this real?"

"Holy…" she tried to say.

"*We* are the end of the rainbow," I whispered.

We looked at each other with wide eyes, then broke into shrieks of glee, like children. The pot-of-gold jokes followed, but in that moment, it was as if we were part of the spiritual world, like the citizens

RAINBOW HILL

Erica Mier

of heaven were watching us, celebrating our discovery, and all of nature was in on it.

As soon as we reached the dorm, I called my mom to tell her what happened. As I predicted, she said what she normally said about rainbows: "Well you know, my daddy always said, 'There's a rainbow after every storm.'"

Not long after Mom moved in with me and Dustin, we sat together after a downpour, and watched a perfect rainbow form end-to-end over the hill behind our house. Within several minutes, one rainbow became two. We soon discovered that our hill had the perfect conditions for double rainbows, and they occurred multiple times a year.

Whenever one of us saw the colors begin, we ran through the house and found anyone who might be home to sit with us on what we eventually began to call "Rainbow Hill." The damp grass soaked the seats of our pants.

When Mom's scleroderma reached the point that she could no longer walk, I pushed her wheelchair to

Erica Mier

the back door so she could look out at Rainbow Hill. She quoted my grandfather again and again, but I never grew tired of hearing, "There's a rainbow after every storm."

***

"When I go, make sure you call the number on Humanities Gifts' business card," she said. "They'll come and pick up my body."

"Ma… I know," I said, mildly annoyed. We'd been over it many times. I knew it was coming, but when she talked this way, it was impossible for me to hide from it. She'd been a nurse most of her life, and decided, because scleroderma was so rare, to donate her body "to science," as she put it.

"But, Mom, where can I go?" I said.

"What?" She looked at me with confusion.

"You know… when you're *gone*."

"I'm still not following."

She never understood the need to visit a place more than once. 'Been there, done that,' she'd say. She preferred new adventures.

RAINBOW HILL

Erica Mier

"Mom, you won't have a grave. And you told me not to waste money on getting your remains cremated. I won't even have ashes to hold onto. So, where am I supposed to go?" I said, tears rolling down my face. "I won't have a place to go, Mama."

She looked at me with mild confusion, but overwhelming love, as if I had missed something so obvious.

"I'll be wherever *you* are," she said.

Her frail hand reached for mine. We sat in silence, and I cried.

The same night, or maybe it was several nights later (so much of her last days are a blur of time, exhaustion, and emotion), I lay in bed and sobbed. Dustin slept beside me soundly, and I tried to muffle my grief. The clock on my phone read 11:37 p.m., and I thought about the work day ahead. Although I adored my eighth-grade students, they were exhausting. I woke up at 5:00 a.m., showered, got dressed, and ran down to Mom's apartment to pour her coffee. She loved the smell. She couldn't drink

RAINBOW HILL

Erica Mier

it, but we still liked to pretend. She was no longer able to get out of bed to use the bathroom on her own, so I changed her adult diaper and hoped she'd be comfortable until her hospice nurse arrived to bathe her. I drove to work, fighting the tears that threatened my mascara, and prayed that my mom would still be alive when I got home.

As midnight approached, I stared at my phone. Dustin was still completely asleep. I needed sleep too, then realized I'd have time to sleep *after*. I pulled myself out of bed and quietly walked down the stairs to Mom's apartment. I walked over to her bed and placed my hand on her shoulder, feeling the soft fleece material of her thin pajamas, which clung to her skeletal frame. It was harder and harder to awaken her, and I wondered if she was actually asleep or moving in and out of consciousness. Her breathing was ragged, and I watched her battle for air, her lungs making a wheezing noise. Sometimes her breathing became so light I placed my hand gently near her nose and mouth to feel it.

RAINBOW HILL

Erica Mier

I climbed into bed beside her tiny frame and felt hot tears roll down my face and neck. She had no awareness I was there, even though the slightest sound from me and my brother when we were little woke her up. My quiet grief turned to body-racking sobs. I wept violently, but still didn't disturb her. I wanted her to awaken with the same strength she had when I was a child running to her bed for comfort after a nightmare. I worried that I would awaken my family upstairs, on the other side of the house, but I couldn't stop myself; I'd lost all control. The woman I tried so hard to protect and shield, who'd once been my protector and shield, was leaving me. My friend. My confidant. My encourager. My travel companion. My burden. My tower of strength. My pain in the ass. My beloved.

I was now realizing my greatest fear: she was actually leaving. I was 11 when my father chose to walk out of our lives. After he left, for the first six months, I would stand at the front door each morning and watch my mom leave for work. I'd wave

RAINBOW HILL

Erica Mier

goodbye, crying and praying to a God I hoped was there.

Please don't let her leave me. She loves me, right? She won't leave too. Please don't take her, God. Please let her come back.

I imagined her in a fatal car accident driving to work, ambulance lights flashing in my mind's eye. I knew she had an autoimmune disease then. *Would she grow sicker at work and never come home to me?*

That 11-year-old girl was now a 36-year-old woman, fearing the same things, crying the same tears. But Mom was still there next to me. I begged God for something different. *Please let me be with her when she leaves.*

My pleas turned to anger. Silently, I heard myself say, *Why did we choose rainbows?* It was foolish. Now it would be impossible to see our sign unless it was daytime. *What if I need you at night? What if I need you on a bright, beautiful day?*

RAINBOW HILL

Erica Mier

My mind continued its rage. Lord God! Will you make me wait for some storm to end so that I *might* get to feel her with me?

But then, it felt like God wanted me to experience this emotional storm, allowing the raging ocean of grief to take hold, casting me about in its powerful and crushing wake. It tossed me around like a powerful wave that breaks over your head, leaving you desperate to find your footing.

My body and soul were weary. Soon, my breaths became more evenly spaced, my sobs like the faint rumble of thunder when a storm finally takes its leave.

It was well after midnight when I managed to gather myself up and crawl out of Mom's bed. I decided to use her bathroom before going upstairs to my bedroom.

Not bothering to turn on the lights, I stepped inside the darkness, guided only by memory and a bit of light from the ceiling fan that quietly rotated in the other room, above Mom's body.

RAINBOW HILL

Erica Mier

Turning the corner, I stopped. My breath caught in my throat. In front of me, in the darkness of her bathroom, were small rainbows illuminating the entire wall. The light from the other room had somehow bounced around the corner, using the bathroom's mirror as a platform. It felt as if the door between heaven and earth had, once again, cracked open just a bit, and this time, it reminded me that the Master Scientist/Artist/Creator would not be bound by my limited expectations of a rainbow.

"Okay, God," I said. "Rainbows it is."

Leaving the bathroom, I walked to Mom's bedside and placed my hand on her frail shoulder. Her chest continued to rise and fall.

"Goodnight, Mama," I said, and kissed her bony cheek. "I love you."

***

Mom took her last breath a week or two after the rainbows appeared on her bathroom wall. I was numb and in a haze of overwhelming grief, but I do know for certain that eleven days passed between the

RAINBOW HILL

Erica Mier

day she died and the day of her funeral. There were
many days when I was driving home and screamed
in my car at the top of my lungs. Then I did it again
until my throat burned. My vision was blurred by
tears, and I pulled the car over and sat shaking
uncontrollably on the side of the road. I knew I
sounded like a lunatic, but it was the only way to
release my overwhelming pain.

In those eleven days after her death, there were
no rainbows.

***

The day of her funeral, the air smelled pungent
and fresh. It was Spring and the warmth of the
sunshine cradled the darkness of my spirit. Outside
my kitchen window were tightly clasped white and
pink dogwood buds, moments away from bursting
into new life – such a contrast, as I prepared to honor
the end of my mother's.

Sunlight danced through the colorful, stained-
glass windows in the church, and I sat in the front

RAINBOW HILL

Erica Mier

row, searching for any hint of a rainbow. Surely a rainbow could appear. But it didn't.

I know I gave her eulogy, I know Dustin also spoke, but I can barely remember it. I know someone read Psalm 23 like she'd requested. When the organist played *Amazing Grace* as background music, I remember laughing through tears as Dustin squeezed my hand. Mom detested *Amazing Grace*, feeling it was too cliché.

Friends and family that I hadn't seen in years surrounded me, but I couldn't give them the attention I wanted to give. I felt barely there. Afterward, we loaded Dustin's trunk with flowers and cards. People approached me to say their goodbyes, but I couldn't focus on anyone. I was so tired. I don't remember the short drive home, or even how I made it upstairs to my bedroom. Normally, I never napped during the day unless I was sick, but those days were not normal.

Dustin entered the room and sat down gently on the bed. "Are you awake?"

RAINBOW HILL

Erica Mier

"Sort of," I said, with no idea how long I'd been asleep.

"I think you need to see something."

I got up and followed Dustin downstairs to where several close friends lingered in our kitchen. He opened the sliding door to our deck and motioned for me to follow him.

"Look," he said, and pointed into the cloudless sky. Shielding my eyes with my hand, I looked up. Through the tree limbs, I first saw the sun.

"Do you see it?" Dustin whispered, smiling and holding my hand.

"No," I said.

"Keep looking," he said, then took off his polarized sunglasses.

Placing them in front of my eyes, I looked into the sky again. To this day, I'm still not sure what we saw; I'd never seen anything like it. The colors of the rainbow were inverted, starting with violet and ending with red; they formed a perfect circle around the sun. The sacred moment had, once again,

RAINBOW HILL

Erica Mier

expanded my perception of rainbows. Wide-eyed, I looked around at my friends. Tears fell from their eyes.

"She did it," I whispered. I could almost hear Mom's proud voice boasting, *Look what I can do now!*

"Not a cloud in the sky," Dustin said, putting his arm around me. "I think she's showing off."

***

In the three years since, her rainbows have appeared everywhere. They appear in photos that I take of my children; they land on my hands coming down through sky lights; at night, when a lamp's light reflects rainbows over my darkened television screen, and they arrive after storms. They appear on days of trial and triumph, and on days I miss her so badly it takes my breath away. I often photograph them, because I need to hold on to the proof. They are her constant reminders: *I'll be wherever you are.*

THE TAPESTRY OF MY YOUTH

Joanne Morley Kalmbach

In 2019, I saw *Beautiful: The Carole King Musical* on Broadway. As I listened to the songs I once knew so well, my 12-year-old inner self returned. Her fear and anger came back too, and the same confusing sensations moved through me, as if I were right back in my bedroom in the '70s. *I feel the earth move under my feet. I feel the sky tumblin' down, a tumblin' down* pounding in my head.

I couldn't keep up with the changes that overtook my family life then. Days and months, then years, revolved around my brother Rudy. He took my parents away from me. They were so busy chasing after him, trying to fix him, they couldn't see me.

***

My sister Tammy tore the *Tapestry* album from its wrapper and said, "Carole King is the coolest." I was 9, and Tammy was 17. I didn't know who Carole King was, but from her picture

THE TAPESTRY OF MY YOUTH

Joanne Morley Kalmbach

on the album cover, sitting in front of a window and holding a blanket, she looked like she could be one of Tammy's friends. She wore jeans and her feet were bare. Her curly hair flowed free. There was a cat by her side.

Tammy and I shared a tiny bedroom in our house in the suburbs of Philadelphia, and I thought she was the coolest, not Carole King. I wanted Tammy's long, dark hair; her platform shoes; bell-bottom jeans; and collection of silver and turquoise rings and bracelets. Right before she played *Tapestry* for me, Tammy had been uptown, hanging out with her girlfriends, something I also didn't have.

Sometimes Tammy was nice, but most of the time she was too busy talking on the phone to even notice me. She usually kicked me out of our room so she could talk to her boyfriend on the phone that our dad installed for *us*. But now, she was inviting me to stay, showing me her new record from the Mad Platter. She'd taken me there once. Hundreds

THE TAPESTRY OF MY YOUTH

Joanne Morley Kalmbach

of albums were stacked like giant playing cards all around the store, and burning incense filled the room. I looked into a big glass case that held little clips with long feathers and miniature glass pipes. I said, "Tammy, will you buy me one of these pretty feathers?" She and the owner of the store looked at each other and burst into laughter. I was angry they were laughing at me, but also glad Tammy had brought me with her.

"Close your eyes and listen to the words – *feel* the music," Tammy said, and placed the scratchy needle on the spinning record. After a few seconds, I wasn't really listening to the words, and wanted to see what Tammy was doing. Slowly, I opened my eyes and saw her in a trance, her eyes still shut. She swayed from side to side, following the rhythm of the music. It seemed to pull her into a different world. And then, eyes closed, she started singing, "I feel the earth move under my feet." At that moment, I wanted to feel the earth move too, but that day, I was finally standing on

THE TAPESTRY OF MY YOUTH

Joanne Morley Kalmbach

solid ground with Tammy. I wasn't her annoying little sister anymore; I was hanging out with my new girlfriend, and I was cooler and older, just like Tammy.

***

"Home Again"

When I was born, my siblings were ages 12, 8, and 6, and being the youngest had its advantages. I was the center of my family's attention. But by the time I reached fifth grade, my brother Rudy and I were the only kids left in the house, and things rapidly changed. Rudy made me laugh, but then he started to scare me. There were days when he wrestled me to the floor and pinned me down, my hands locked behind my back.

"No, don't do it," I told him and laughed when he threatened to spit on me. Instead of stopping, he coughed up a big loogie and let it drip down his chin. I kicked and shook my head from side to side, desperately trying to break free, but he overpowered me.

THE TAPESTRY OF MY YOUTH

Joanne Morley Kalmbach

"Mommy! Mommy! Help me!" I shouted.

"Rudy, get off her!" Mom yelled, running into the room. He held his spit over my face until the last second, sucking it back in before he released me from his grip. I ran and hid in my room, unsure of what else Rudy might do to me.

He convinced my parents, after eight years in Catholic school, to let him go to public high school. No more school uniforms for him; he wore black greaser boots, a black leather jacket, jeans, and a chain wallet. His dark locks hung beneath his motorcycle helmet, and when he revved up his bike in the street, the whole neighborhood knew he was home.

"So Far Away"

By the time I was in seventh grade, my parents tried to pretend everything was okay in our house. Rudy was out of high school but still living at home, although he was hardly ever there. He left for days, sometimes weeks, at a time. When he returned, he locked himself in his room, and slept for days.

THE TAPESTRY OF MY YOUTH

Joanne Morley Kalmbach

"Mom, why does Rudy sleep so much?" I asked.

"I guess he's just really tired," she said.

But I knew about Rudy's drug addiction. I figured it out on my own, piecing it together after overhearing his violent arguments with my parents.

"Rudy, we found drugs in your room again today."

"Then stay the hell out of my room, and you won't find any!" Rudy shouted.

His threatening, erratic behavior became more and more pronounced, and I feared his highs and lows, afraid of what he might do to himself, of what he might do to my parents and me. I had no one to talk to about it. At 12, trying to fit in at school was hard enough without talking about what was happening at home.

When Rudy was gone, Mom had time to snuggle with me on the sofa. We ate Twizzlers and watched The Brady Bunch and Love American

THE TAPESTRY OF MY YOUTH

Joanne Morley Kalmbach

Style, two of my favorite shows, but we never talked about the chaos. It felt good just to sit and comfort one another. It seemed she needed these moments as much as I did. We both knew our calmness could turn to unpredictable madness.

"It's Too Late"

"Rudy!" I yelled, banging on the door of our only bathroom. "I need to go. You've been in there forever! Open the door!"

"Leave me alone!" he shouted at me. Mom and Dad raced up the stairs.

"What is going on?"

"He's been in there for at least an hour, and he won't come out."

Dad knocked on the door.

"Rudy, what's going on? Are you okay?"

"Go way! Leave me alone!"

"Please open the door. What are you doing?"

"Leave me 'lone!" he spat, growing angrier.

"I'm shaving! Shaving!"

THE TAPESTRY OF MY YOUTH

Joanne Morley Kalmbach

The bathroom door doesn't have a lock. Dad tried to open it, but it slammed back in his face.

Mom cried and screamed and pulled me down the hallway while Dad and Rudy played tug of war with the door. After a few minutes, Dad finally won, and the door swung open. Rudy held a razor, his whole face covered in blood. It dripped down his face and neck.

Mom ran to him. "Rudy, what have you done?" I could tell from his eyes that he was high.

"I'm just shaving!" he screamed. "What's wrong with you?!?"

He pushed us aside, made it to his room, and slammed the door. I went outside and sat alone on the porch and cried. Fifteen minutes later, I saw a car pull up and park on the side of our house. The horn beeped twice. Within seconds, Rudy ran out the front door and jumped into the passenger seat.

He never noticed me sitting on the porch, and the car sped away.

THE TAPESTRY OF MY YOUTH

Joanne Morley Kalmbach

***

Later, I learn from my parents that they made him roll up his sleeves, looking for track marks. They don't find any that day. Crack cocaine is now his drug of choice. I also learn that Rudy was hallucinating. As he shaved in the bathroom, he saw more hair appear. He kept shaving and shaving, trying to remove it.

I try to fall asleep that night, but I hear both my parents crying in their bedroom. This will be the first of many nights I'll hear them cry. I'll also hear them argue about how to fix their son. Should they try "tough love" with Rudy, or should they find other ways to help him?

I need to drown out the crying. Tammy left her turntable when she moved out, and most of her records. I search through what's left and come across *Tapestry*. I carefully set the needle down and walk back to my bed. I'm completely alone, and I hear the words of the songs like it's the very first time, like Tammy never played the record

THE TAPESTRY OF MY YOUTH

Joanne Morley Kalmbach

over and over, eventually growing tired of it and leaving it behind. It's as though Carole King wrote every song just for me.

The music calms me down and I can finally sleep. For the first time, I don't feel alone. I spend many, many nights in 1974 and 1975 feeling like I have a friend in Carole King.

***

"Joanne, it's time to go. Are you ready?" Mom yells. A year has passed, and I run downstairs and out the door and climb into the back seat of my dad's light-blue Cadillac. It's Sunday afternoon, the only day visitors are permitted. Every Sunday, after church, we change our clothes and drive an hour to Kensington, one of the worst parts of Philadelphia. The streets are lined with drug addicts passed out on stoops. I wonder if Dad recognizes some of the faces from when he was searching for Rudy the year before. We pass drug deals on street corners. Dad parks our car on a side

THE TAPESTRY OF MY YOUTH

Joanne Morley Kalmbach

street and locks the doors. I'm sure he's wondering if the car will be there after our two-hour visit.

We walk quickly around the corner and down the side street to the inpatient rehab center. Rudy was in and out of four or five rehabs before this one. No one's allowed to visit during the first three months. Finally, we could visit him, and he looked different. I saw a little bit of his old self in him, the brother I wasn't afraid of, but he shook. Now, three months later, he looks like I remember him before his addiction. He's put on weight, and his eyes are clear. He has a big smile on his face when he sees us enter the room. We're all smiling. I know life won't be the same again, for any of us, but it feels like we're finally on the right path. I feel the earth stand still beneath my feet, like it did when Tammy first played *Tapestry* for me. It feels good. We're not running from each other, and I don't feel invisible anymore.

THE TAPESTRY OF MY YOUTH

Joanne Morley Kalmbach

"I've been telling everyone here how much I miss your homemade sauce and pasta," Rudy says to Mom.

"How about I make enough for everyone here? We'll bring it next Sunday," Mom says.

"You would do that?"

"Of course! I'd do anything for you."

I take this moment in. I want Rudy to realize that Mom and Dad *did* do everything for him. I fear the drugs have ruined his memory and he doesn't realize how far they went to save him. He might not remember how scared we were. I start to ask him if he remembers, but he interrupts me.

"And how about you, li'l sis? You want to play a game of pool with me?"

"You bet!" I say.

"But don't cry if I beat you this time."

We smile at each other and walk over to the pool table. I decide not to bring up the past.

***

THE TAPESTRY OF MY YOUTH

Joanne Morley Kalmbach

In the '70s, many of Rudy's "friends" died from overdoses, so I do not fault my parents for trying to help "fix" my brother. I don't blame them for forcing him into rehab, even though he repeatedly ran away and refused help. I don't blame my father for driving through the worst parts of Philadelphia, risking his own life, looking for him. Those decisions were made out of love, and the fear of permanently losing their son to addiction. My parents were also trying to survive what Rudy's addiction did to their relationship.

There was no such thing in those days (or at least they didn't know about it) as support groups for families or siblings of addicts. My parents thought the best way to protect me from Rudy's addiction was to try and keep it from me. I thought it would be even harder and more painful for my parents if I asked questions, so I stayed silent. Younger siblings of addicts are often silent victims, neglected in the storm, without outlets or ways to express their pain. My parents didn't have

THE TAPESTRY OF MY YOUTH

Joanne Morley Kalmbach

the resources or the finances to get me, or themselves, the help we all needed. Addiction brings unnerving tension and chaos into a home, and home is a place where a child should feel safe. Rudy and his addiction took that from me.

Even though my adolescence was tumultuous and out of control, I never doubted that my parents loved me unconditionally, just like they loved Rudy.

Today, I know my mom and dad saved my brother's life. If not for them, I know he would have overdosed. They never gave up on him. As a parent, I now understand the choices they were forced to make. I too would do anything to save my child. As much as my parents saved my brother, I like to think that I helped save them. When Rudy was gone, they couldn't stay in bed all day and cry. Because of me, they had to *get up every morning with smiles on their faces*. I know I brought them light and joy during their darkest days. Together, we learned to finally stand still –

THE TAPESTRY OF MY YOUTH

Joanne Morley Kalmbach

we were no longer chasing Rudy's addiction. In the end, love ended our madness.

> *"I have often asked myself the reason*
> *for the sadness in a world*
> *where tears are just a lullaby.*
> *If there's any answer, maybe*
> *love can end the madness.*
> *Maybe not, oh, but we can only try."*

-- Carole King, "Beautiful"

AN UNLIKELY ANGEL

Pat Muccigrosso

The first blush of light touches the December sky. Here, in this concrete canyon, it is hard to tell what hour of the day it is, but you and I know. It is time.

"Good morning." The nurse walks to your side. "Can you tell me your name and date of birth, please?"

How many times have you been asked that question in the last 12 months? I peel myself away from your side and slide out of bed. Scanning your wristband, she smiles. "The OR team is on its way." You stay just where you are.

"Come on, grumble bunny." I lean in to hug you. "Time to get up."

They arrive in their crepe-sole shoes, clipboards in hand. We keep smiles glued to our faces and whisper gently to each other while the OR team buzzes around us, intent on their tasks, unlocking wheels, tying up IV lines, and checking your chart against your wrist band.

The anesthesiologist bounds into the already crowded room, blue scrubs hugging his lanky frame,

AN UNLIKELY ANGEL

Pat Muccigrosso

a goofy grin on his face. "I'm Dr. Rand. I'll be putting you under." He glances at his watch. "In about 10 minutes. Time to go!"

They are ready now. I am not. I lean down to hug you one last time. I kiss your cheek and touch your arm.

"I love you, babe." I step back as they wheel the bed around and start for the door.

"I love you too," you say, smiling. You reach for me.

"I'm going to walk with you to the operating room," I whisper. I am holding your hand. I am holding my breath. If I breathe, if I try to talk, I'll shatter. I can feel it.

I cannot take another step. I stop and tell you with the last bit of air in my lungs that I love you and will be waiting for you. They push on. Your fingers slip from mine, pulled away, as the gurney continues down the hall. You wave, just as you round the corner, and I turn away.

AN UNLIKELY ANGEL

Pat Muccigrosso

It's as though someone has punched me. I can't catch my breath. What is wrong with me? I've been so strong for so many months, but I feel like I'm shattering. Standing alone in your now-empty hospital room, the walls close in.

***

August 7, 1991: the beach, a weekend with friends, our 17th wedding anniversary. Pat got food poisoning, or so we thought, until blood streamed into the toilet and he doubled over in pain. In the Emergency Room that night, I joked that this was an anniversary I would never forget. I haven't. It's etched in my mind.

Shuffling around the corner of his desk, Dr. Cerrone wouldn't make eye contact with us when we met with him. Waving the piece of paper in his hand, he said, "I have your biopsy results."

Pat didn't move so I took the paper from the doctor's outstretched hand. I couldn't make out any of the words on the page. I offered the paper to Pat, but his eyes were fixed on Dr. Cerrone's face.

AN UNLIKELY ANGEL

Pat Muccigrosso

"I'm sorry," I finally said. "I'm not sure what I'm looking at."

Staring at something over my left shoulder, Dr. Cerrone coughed, then looked down at his desk. He spoke so softly I had to ask him to repeat it.

"You have cancer, Mr. Muccigrosso."

I grabbed Pat's hand, tears welling in my eyes. Pat didn't move. He didn't even blink. It was as though he was frozen in place. Dr. Cerrone's voice finally cut through the silence.

"I'm sorry. It's high-stage. And high-grade. You need immediate surgery," he said, and looked at me, not Pat. "I've scheduled you for tomorrow."

"Me?" I said, and shook my head.

"No, not you, your husband," Dr. Cerrone said, but continued to stare at me while he spoke. "We can discuss chemotherapy after we operate."

"Will the surgery get all the cancer?" I asked.

"There are no guarantees, but there's only one tumor, and it looks like it will be easy to remove," he said. "It looks pretty good, but no guarantees."

AN UNLIKELY ANGEL

Pat Muccigrosso

Walking out of the doctor's office, I held Pat's hand. "It's going to be okay, babe. Surgery tomorrow, a week off work then back to normal, right?" I grinned.

Nodding, Pat got into the car, and we drove home to get ready for the next day.

That's how we jumped on the merry-go-round of modern healthcare. But Pat and I were so naïve, believing it was a one and done and our lives would go on as before, easily, comfortably, happily. But they didn't. The cancer returned. Pat had a second surgery just before Thanksgiving, and another course of chemo.

"Maybe this time," we whispered to each other, lying together as dawn broke. Maybe this time, it would be over. But it wasn't, not that time, or the next time, or the next. Seven surgeries later, almost a year after the diagnosis, we sat across the desk from Dr. Cerrone again. "You've got another tumor," he said. Glancing at his calendar, humming softly under

AN UNLIKELY ANGEL

Pat Muccigrosso

his breath, he found a slot and penciled-in our last name. "Another surgery, I'm afraid."

"No. Not again," I heard myself say. Pat's head turned slowly toward me. "Not with you."

My voice rose with anger as I stood up. "Look at him, Dr. Cerrone! Really look at him!" I took Pat's hand. "He can't take much more, and frankly, neither can I."

Dr. Cerrone stood up. His mouth opened, then, just as quickly, closed. He sat back down. "I told you there were no guarantees. You remember me saying that, right? I didn't make any promises. Look, I think you're right. I think I've done all I can do. There's a doctor in Philadelphia who might be able to help. I'll refer you."

And with those words, he walked out of his office, and we moved into Phase II with a new doctor, a new plan, and maybe a different outcome.

With medical records, a series of imaging disks, and our courage, Pat and I headed for Philadelphia to meet the doctor who wrote the book on bladder

AN UNLIKELY ANGEL

Pat Muccigrosso

cancer. It was October; the weather was cold and bleak, all blacks and browns and grays outside, and just as bleak inside.

"It's spread," Dr. Gamella said, his face worn from all the times he'd had to tell someone the same bad news. "Your bladder has to come out."

Nodding, blinking, we waited for this man, who held our future in his hands, to tell us the rest.

"The surgery will be extensive. Your prostate, your lymph glands, they all have to come out, too." He paused and waited for us to catch up. *Such a kind face*, I thought. *He's done this so many times before.* He had more bad news, but he knew we were struggling to hear him, to fully understand him, so he waited.

"Sooner rather than later," he finally said.

"You'll come in the day before so we can start early."

We didn't cry this time. There was no reprieve, no miracle cure, only one aggressive, surgical, life-changing way forward. This surgery. This day. This

AN UNLIKELY ANGEL

Pat Muccigrosso

place. This empty hospital room where they left me standing – alone.

My knees buckle. I slide to the floor. I rock back and forth, wrapping my arms around myself as the room fades away. The sounds in the hallway – beeping IVs, murmuring nurses, pages for doctors, patient call bells – all fall silent, disappearing as I close my eyes and weep.

By myself, stranded on this island, nothing gets through to me except one sound, slowly and surely rising, growing stronger and louder. Opening my eyes, I look around for the source of this awful, keening howl. It cuts the air like the cry of a dying animal.

And then I realize it's me. I fall from a great height into a deep abyss, fall so rapidly I barely notice the housekeeper slip into the room. She's a fixture, like the wall-mounted television and the furniture, a stranger, a woman with a mop and rag and endless rooms to clean.

AN UNLIKELY ANGEL

Pat Muccigrosso

Silently, she moves to my side and enfolds me in her arms. I'm flying apart, but still, she holds me tightly, watching with her amber eyes, soothing with her touch, saying nothing, which is all I need to hear.

She waits for me to stop wailing and start breathing again. She helps me to my feet, holds me gently, and sings words in a language I don't understand.

Slowly, I return to the room, to her voice. I focus on her face, her beautiful face. It's as though she is lit from within, glowing with life and love. Her golden-brown eyes, so deep, so gentle, and so willing to hold my sorrow and pain.

I hug her fiercely, resting in the sweet feeling of peace pouring out of her. I let out a small breath of air and, with it, all the fear and sorrow of the last year leaves my body. How long we stand there, I don't know.

When the nurse steps into the room, she's towing a priest behind her, someone she thought could help

AN UNLIKELY ANGEL

Pat Muccigrosso

me. "This is Father Kelly," she says, staring at the housekeeper. "He'll take it from here."

We pull apart, the housekeeper and I. She tries to leave the room as quietly as she came in. I push the priest away, run after her, and cry, "Wait!" I touch her arm. "I don't even know your name."

"I am Ahn." Her fingers graze my cheek. Music, far away but very clear, fills my head. Voices of angels, intertwined with chanting monks and chiming temple bells, swell inside me. My soul, resonating with the glorious sound, fills with light and love.

"That's Vietnamese, isn't it?" The priest's voice cuts through the heavenly symphony. "It means 'peace,' I think."

"Ahn," I sigh, and breathed out. *Ahn.*

She smiles and holds me in her gaze. The golden glow that radiates from her transfixes me, filling me, filling the room with light and energy.

"I was over there, you know," the priest says, stepping closer. "In the '60s, I mean -- the war."

AN UNLIKELY ANGEL

Pat Muccigrosso

Ahn backs away. "I must go. I have work to do."

"No! Wait," I cry. "Don't go. Please."

Looking into my eyes, she doesn't speak, but I hear her voice anyway, ringing like a small crystal bell in my head. "Do not fear, đứa bé. I will be with you always, even unto the ends of the earth." Bowing slightly, she leaves the room.

I watch as she walks down the hall, but I'm not afraid anymore. I know I'm not alone.

I've never believed in angels, but I met one that morning. She is with me, still.

FULL CIRCLE

Jolene Wilson-Glah

"This baby is coming right now," my mother said, through the pain. "Get the nurse!" My father sprinted out of the scrub room, turning out the light on his way. When he returned with the red-haired American nurse, my mother had already delivered me herself, breech, in the dark.

While I may have arrived in this world feet first, it was many years before I felt grounded in my family. My relationship with my mother was a complicated one, which I've only come to understand, and appreciate, in the seven years since her death.

***

My parents were both working for Trans World Airlines (TWA) when they met. Dad, already an executive with TWA, came to the Philadelphia office to conduct an audit. Mom was a ticket agent. She was Lauren Bacall-beautiful, with a tall, straight bearing, and blonde, wavy hair she often wore tied in a satin ribbon. After repeated lunch and dinner invitations

FULL CIRCLE

Jolene Wilson-Glah

on Dad's part (all declined), he returned to see her one last time, and Mom finally accepted.

"Even though I'd been flirting with the possibility of accepting Chill Lindsey's proposal, your dad represented a better long-term prospect," she later revealed to me.

So, on the cusp of age 25, not having seen my father for many months, Mom boldly flew alone to meet him in Central America. They were married in the small chapel of the Metropolitan Cathedral in San José, Costa Rica. Mom's international life with Daddy would span almost a decade; quite a departure for a girl from center-city Philadelphia, the only daughter of a beat cop and a seamstress, with four competitive, younger brothers.

After several international assignments, my parents arrived in Ethiopia in 1948. I was born there, two years later. They led privileged lives during these years. There was a nanny for me and a different one for my older brother, a cook, a gardener, and a house boy. I remember the maroon brocade silk from

FULL CIRCLE

Jolene Wilson-Glah

Paris that Daddy bought for Mom. She had the fabric fashioned into a flowing gown for her first dinner party at the palace of Emperor Haile Selassie.

"I felt like a princess as I bowed to the emperor," Mom said. She was 30 years old. And every time I heard the stories and imagined her at those dinners, I thought of Deborah Kerr in *The King and I*. All of these images presented an enchanting view of life, and one that I wanted for myself, just like Mom.

I saw the photos from their garden parties on the manicured lawn, where uniformed, white-gloved servants brought the guests free-flowing gin and tonics and finger foods. Tables with crisp, white linens were scattered under trees that filled the air with the pungent, earthy smell of eucalyptus. Mom loved entertaining and later taught me the fine art of setting a table.

After eight years in Africa and a stop in Rome for a private audience with Pope Pius XII, our family returned to the States. My father left his executive position with TWA and opened a business with two

FULL CIRCLE

Jolene Wilson-Glah

of my mother's brothers. My parents settled into a pleasant, but perhaps somewhat boring, life on a farm.

Daddy whistled as he cut the grass on his red John Deere tractor with scary-looking wheels, pulling an even scarier looking sickle behind it. The unmistakable, damp scent of freshly cut hay tickled my nose. Mom, going from princess to mistress of her own estate, seemed to slip seamlessly into a quiet, country life.

But on a sticky summer day, I followed my older brother Mark up to the barn to "help" him polish the family car, a behemoth grey Studebaker. The sweat ran in rivulets down my neck. I asked my brother if I could have a sip of the Coke he gulped from a dripping, cold, green bottle. "No," he answered.

Asserting my independence, I found a nearby container, walked to the farm spigot, which towered over me, and filled the container to the top with water. I greedily drank it down. I didn't know that the can contained the remainder of the car polish.

FULL CIRCLE

Jolene Wilson-Glah

Soon my stomach cramped and I ran to tell Mom. Sitting in an orange chair on the front porch, she was putting the finishing touches on a baby-blue sweater she'd knitted for me.

"Woody!" Mom screamed, "Hurry! We need to get Jolene to the hospital. She drank something."

She bundled me in the sweater and Daddy drove us to the small local hospital, his eyes riveted on the winding country roads. When we arrived, Mom sat silently in the emergency room, holding me tightly in that soft blue sweater. Daddy went into action after talking to the doctor, swaddling me in a sheet. He held me down and softly cooed in my ear while the doctors shoved a tube down my nose. He cuddled me, rubbed my head, and continued his soothing whispers as we rode the elevator to the corner crib in the children's ward. As I looked through the bars of the crib at Daddy's retreating back, I did not see my mother. I have no memory of her there, not her voice or her face. While I felt abandoned by her then, I see

FULL CIRCLE

Jolene Wilson-Glah

now, after becoming a mother myself, that the thought of losing a child likely terrified her.

My sister, Ruthie, was born about two years later. I was almost five. My parents brought her home from the hospital, and Mom explained to me, while feeding her, "I had to have another baby, because I need a baby to raise." I wondered: *Where do I fit now? What is my place? How can I stand out?*

Mark was the oldest, Ruthie was the baby for Mom to raise, and I decided to be the strong and independent one, just like Mom. My mantra became, "I can do it by my own big self."

I was eight when I first noticed Mom practicing the daily ritual of changing her clothes, putting on lipstick, and carefully dabbing a few drops of exotic and pungent *Joy* perfume behind her ears before Daddy got home. When I asked her why she did that, she turned and said, "Because I know your father does not have to come home to me every day." Somehow, I understood what she meant and the importance of that ritual. Not only would I need to be

FULL CIRCLE

Jolene Wilson-Glah

strong and independent, I had to be feminine and fashionable too.

When it came time for my parent's annual Christmas cocktail party, I watched how Mom put the party together with the ease of a magician, producing elaborate appetizers in the time it takes most people to make a peanut-butter-and-jelly sandwich. After she meticulously set the table with our gold-rimmed china, etched crystal, and silver trays laden with food, she disappeared into her bedroom. She soon reappeared at the top of the stairs, dressed in something elegant and festive: a purple jumpsuit, with billowing green, purple, and gold sleeves. Her signature scent of tuberose and spice floated down the stairway as she descended. When she joined my dad in the living room, I saw the pride in his eyes. I wanted to be a woman who would garner that kind of love and pride from a man when I grew up.

One spring afternoon, when I was fourteen, Mom and I walked in downtown Philadelphia, holding

FULL CIRCLE

Jolene Wilson-Glah

hands. I wore a blue, Audrey Hepburn-style dress, stockings with a girdle, kitten heels, and white gloves. Mom bought me a broad-brimmed, navy blue hat at Wanamaker's; it turned up on one side and had a large bow in the back. It was my princess look. Mom stood back and smiled at me, and I stole glimpses of our reflections in the store windows as we walked. I was finally part of her stylish, glamorous world.

Mom insisted I take modeling lessons. She drove me to photo shoots and fashion layouts, and she joined me in newspaper ads. At sixteen, I entered and won the county Junior Miss pageant. When they pinned the sash across my dress, placed a crown on my head, and took pictures for the newspaper, Mom posed proudly beside me. I felt strong, fashionable, admired, and accepted by my mother; my position in the family was secure.

Sundays were family days, which usually meant all five of us -- Mom, Dad, Mark, Ruthie and me -- reading together in the living room while listening to

FULL CIRCLE

Jolene Wilson-Glah

classical music from the Philadelphia Orchestra. Daddy and I took up our usual spots on the small, green sofa, facing the fireplace. He sat at one end, and I lay on my back with my head in his lap as we read. Those warm, cozy Sunday afternoons came to an abrupt end the day Mom stepped into the living room and stopped dead in the opening of the French doors, holding a plate of homemade fudge.

"Jolene!" she said. "Aren't you a little old for that?"

Shame filled my body. It was as though I was no longer her daughter -- I was her competitor.

I didn't share another Sunday afternoon with my family, and Daddy no longer came to my room to say good night. Everything changed. The closeness that I'd finally established with my mother disappeared.

The rest of my teenage years were filled with confusion, and Mom encouraged me to date any boy who asked. One of those boys was Thomas, an exchange student from Norway. I fancied myself madly in love with him, and, after high school, I also

FULL CIRCLE

Jolene Wilson-Glah

became an exchange student and moved to Sweden to be close to him.

Once again, I was trying to win my mother's approval by emulating her independence and boldness, traveling abroad like she did as a young adult.

When that year in Sweden ended, Thomas went into the military, and I went home to attend college. Now that I was "worldly," college soon bored me, and I started searching for my next adventure. I looked around and thought, *Well, I've lived in Europe; I've been to college* (even though, it was only a semester). *What's next?* Marriage, I decided. So, at nineteen, I married a man I barely knew. He was a PhD candidate at Princeton and a "good, long-term prospect," which I thought was expected in a husband.

When my father died at age 62, I was 26 and living in Texas. I was angry at my dad for years after his death; he'd left me with the parent who did not love me, because it was clear to me that my brother

FULL CIRCLE

Jolene Wilson-Glah

was Mom's favorite. She told me as much at my nephew's wedding: "I have always known exactly what Mark was feeling and experiencing. We have had an unbreakable bond."

My sister Ruthie was also close to Mom, and she became her travel companion after Dad died, until Mom remarried. Ruthie and her family lived closer to Mom than I did, and they were together often.

Over the years, I saw my mother infrequently. I finished college and law school, had a daughter, divorced my PhD husband, opened my own, successful law practice, and married Thomas, my long-lost love from Norway. I traveled the world with him.

But, when I was 32, and building my own home, I reached out to my mother and asked for help with a small, short-term loan. She refused.

"You don't need my help," was her explanation.

Tears streamed silently down my cheeks as I said, "Okay, Mom, I understand." I hung up the phone and sobbed. I wasn't brave enough to tell her

FULL CIRCLE

Jolene Wilson-Glah

the truth. *You are so wrong*, I should have said. *I need you very much, and not just for help with money.*

All the while, I knew she bought my brother and sister their own houses. She mistook my strength and independence for not needing her in my life, and I didn't know how to communicate with her, how to tell her that I loved her, and how lonely I felt without her.

It wasn't until her 90th birthday party that I began to understand what life was really like for her, growing up in Philadelphia. The whole family was gathered in California to celebrate, and at dinner that night, she mused, "I would live my life again exactly as I have, except I would have gone to college. I should have, you know. I was smarter than all my brothers." I asked her that day what made her such a strong woman. She turned, looked intently into my eyes, and answered, "In my family, we had no choice." I wonder now if she also made a conscious decision to be "strong and independent," like I did, to secure a respected place within her family.

FULL CIRCLE

Jolene Wilson-Glah

Then, I was diagnosed with stage 4 cancer at age 61. I was terrified to tell her, afraid she'd think I'd somehow failed. When I did tell her, she just stared ahead. Finally, I heard her say, "I am so sorry."

Mom arranged a champagne dinner with family and friends when I took charge of the inevitable and shaved my head. It felt as though she was acknowledging both my bravery and my vulnerability, and I no longer needed to be strong and independent to earn her love and acceptance.

Because my childhood mantra had been *I'll do it by my own big self,* I initially resisted her participation in my journey with cancer. I registered for my first chemo treatment and heard a timid, frail voice behind me say, "Jolene, I'm here."

I turned and saw a different mother standing there. Mom looked small and frightened, wearing a white coat and a matching white beret (always the fashionable one). She awkwardly clutched a black purse I'd given her years before. Inside were carefully ironed, cotton hankies. I never knew if they

FULL CIRCLE

Jolene Wilson-Glah

were for me or for her. Maybe they were for both of us.

She sat beside me during every chemo treatment. She brought me cookies and Coke to ease the nausea. She tucked the sheets around me and gave me a fluffy robe to warm my shrinking body, a turban for my bald head. She wrapped me in a hand-knitted prayer shawl -- "To keep you safe," she said.

Two years later, as Mom lay in a hospice bed in an induced coma, I carefully tucked a patchwork family quilt, generations-old, around her shrunken frame. I hoped it would keep *her* warm and safe. A month earlier, she'd been lucid and knew I'd broken my shoulder.

"Oh, Jolene," she said, "I am so sorry I cannot take care of you." I assured her that I would spend my recovery at her home and her nurse could care for both of us.

On November 5, 2013, before checking in to have my shoulder surgery, I visited Mom at the hospice room in the new wing of the hospital, where

FULL CIRCLE

Jolene Wilson-Glah

she'd been since the previous week. I whispered, "Mom, when Ruthie picks me up today, after my surgery, I'll go to your house. I'll sleep in your bed, and your nurse will take care of me for you." Even in a coma, I felt she heard me. I thought I saw her smile.

When Ruthie picked me up and we'd arrived at Mom's house that evening, the phone rang. Ruthie answered the call and she became very quiet.

"Thank you for letting us know," she said, and set the phone down. She looked over at me. "Mom's gone."

We were forced to make immediate arrangements with the funeral home. Despite being woozy from surgery, I was in "get it done" mode for a few hours. Later, after Ruthie left, the reality of my loss fell over me like a heavy blanket. I felt small, scared, like a child again.

"Mom!" I cried. "Not yet! I'm not ready to lose you!"

***

FULL CIRCLE

Jolene Wilson-Glah

Now, almost eight years later, I'm finally able to express what I wasn't brave enough to say when my mother was alive:

Mom, we still have so much to learn and love about one another. I finally understand that Dad didn't leave me with the parent who did not love me. He left me with a parent who loved me unconditionally – the one who wanted nothing more than to know me and have me know her. I wish I could have seen the real you earlier in my life, Mom. It might have made all the difference. I love you.

A LOVELY LIGHT

Maryellen Winkler

Somewhere in high school, shortly after I decided that I wanted to be a writer, I hit a roadblock: all of my "hero writers" were men. I had just finished *Great Expectations* and thought it was the most engrossing story ever written. Charles Dickens quickly became my favorite author. Then I discovered Matthew Arnold, who became my favorite poet. Arnold's "Dover Beach" spoke to my fifteen-year-old soul.

It was the 1950s and the inequalities that existed in society troubled me. I was not as beautiful as the women I saw on television, and it seemed to me that only physical beauty determined "success" for women. We were not valued for our thoughts and accomplishments. My mind boiled over with questions about love and life. How should I go about being valued as a person and not a stereotype? How did the spiritual mind imbue the physical body?

My older brother, Paul, whose college textbook had introduced me to Arnold's writing, encouraged

A LOVELY LIGHT

Maryellen Winkler

my questions. Paul saw how I was questioning everything, and he pointed me in the direction of Eastern writings, such as the *Bhagavad Gita*. I must admit I struggled with the *Gita*, but I understood its larger message, which encouraged spiritual enlightenment. Paul also taught me to play the guitar. Armed with this tool of self-expression, I wrote songs and short poems about my search for meaning.

My teenage girlfriends did not share my interest in songwriting, Eastern philosophy, poetry, and yoga. Their concerns were more immediate – boyfriends, clothes, and school. If I'd said, "What's your opinion of reincarnation?" they would have looked at me as if I were crazy, and avoided me in the future.

When Paul left Delaware to live in Arizona, I felt like the speaker in "Dover Beach," existing in a "world, which… hath really neither joy, nor love, nor light, nor certitude, nor peace, nor help for pain." I longed to write deep-down, soul-searching words like these that expressed my alienation from the

A LOVELY LIGHT

Maryellen Winkler

materialism of modern society and its emphasis on Barbie-doll beauty. I worried, though, that because I wasn't a man, I wouldn't be able to write meaningful poetry, and no one would take me seriously.

With Paul gone, there was no one else to talk to. My mother would have dismissed my thoughts as frivolous. Religion and duty to tradition were her first concerns. The nuns at my Catholic high school were also unapproachable.

I looked around for a respected woman poet I could emulate. This was 30 years before Maya Angelou recited "On the Pulse of Morning" at the first inauguration of Bill Clinton, and 55 years before Amanda Gorman captivated the world with her poem "The Hill We Climb" at the inauguration of Joseph Biden, just two weeks after a deadly mob attacked the U.S. Capitol.

In 1963, hoping to encourage my writing, my mother offered me her copy of Anne Morrow Lindbergh's *Gift from the Sea*. After a quick perusal, I didn't feel particularly inspired by it. Then I tried

A LOVELY LIGHT

Maryellen Winkler

Emily Dickinson, but I didn't take to her either. Her poetry was clever, but lacked action and emotion.

There were few places for a 15-year-old girl to encounter women writers in 1963. We never studied them in school. The closest I ever came to finding any other genre of art that touched me was when I listened to my first Joan Baez album and heard the words to the sweetly mournful Child Ballads by Francis James Child. Here was love and loss, young women mourning unfaithful lovers or escaping bad husbands. But none of the women in the ballads were authors.

Could women write as well as men? I wondered. Were my feelings even valid, given that I couldn't find them reflected in the works of the few female poets I had read? I worried that my feelings were adolescent drivel, not worthy of expression.

Then, in 1965, when I was 17, I received a book of poetry as a Christmas gift from my parents: *The Collected Poems of Edna St. Vincent Millay*. Her poems were erudite, yet full of the yearning and

A LOVELY LIGHT

Maryellen Winkler

sadness that young women feel. In her I found my literary soulmate.

I was thrilled to discover she won the Pulitzer Prize for poetry in 1923, and was the first woman to do so. There was hope! I took her book to college with me in 1966, and littered it with small pieces of paper to mark the pages of my favorite poems.

At the University of Delaware, I became aware of how racism and the Jim Crow South were rising up to defeat the efforts of Dr. King and other civil rights activists. Overcome with thoughts of his assassination in 1968, I scribbled poetry late into the night. Walking beneath the beauty of the autumn trees that lined South Campus, it felt like I was in an alien landscape. How could such loveliness exist in a world that murdered those who fought for equality and justice?

My roommate patiently listened to some of my poems, but like my earlier girlfriends, she wasn't really interested. When she teased me for staying up late, I quoted my muse Millay:

A LOVELY LIGHT

Maryellen Winkler

"My candle burns at both ends;
It will not last the night;
But ah, my foes, and oh, my friends—
It gives a lovely light."

But before I finished speaking, she was asleep.

I sent some of my poems to the campus literary magazine. When they finally published one, in the spring of 1969, a year after MLK's assassination, I bought five copies of the magazine for my family and friends.

"Autumn"
Brilliant blue the backdrop
And golden glows the light
Dazzling rubies, emeralds, topaz
Deep browns hold upright.
Warmth they wear with happiness
And life beats hope to hold

A LOVELY LIGHT

Maryellen Winkler

But see the marble naked white
A girl now hard and cold.

In the '70s, after I graduated college, I was caught up in the folk movement and devoted my free time to singing and writing songs. Busy working and caring for my husband and child, I still felt that my calling was to be a writer, so I worked a variety of part-time retail jobs to allow myself time to write. But money was tight at home, and I accepted a full-time job as a legal secretary. Still, I sent my best songs to be copyrighted, and even sent a few to music publishers who rejected them. My husband said, "You're living in a fantasy world, Maryellen." I reread Millay's own words about struggle and heartache and wasn't discouraged.

> *"Love is not all: it is not meat nor drink*
> *Nor slumber nor a roof against the rain;*
> *Nor yet a floating spar to men that sink*
> *And rise and sink and rise and sink again."*

A LOVELY LIGHT

Maryellen Winkler

By the '80s, I was a mother for the second time and could afford to stay home for a few years. That's when I discovered Erma Bombeck. I read her column and thought, *I can do this; I'm a wife and mother.* I tried to emulate Bombeck's skewed take on the travails of parenthood with essays on the shortage of good babysitters (mine threw parties and then threw up on the stairs) and the never-ending drudge of housework. I sent several of them to Delaware's main newspaper, the *News Journal*, which accepted and published them. I was grateful for the recognition, but even more grateful for the boost in confidence. Then financial need raised its head again, and I returned to full-time employment, working for Chase Manhattan Bank. With a full-time job and two children, there was no time left in my day for writing.

Around the same time, I found a new literary love: mystery novels. I devoured them during my lunch hour, hunched over my sandwich with the latest P.D. James. Here was a genre made up of many

A LOVELY LIGHT

Maryellen Winkler

women writers, women who published under their own name, women who won awards, and women recognized for their talent. These awards validated the hard work I knew women writers must do in order to be taken seriously, and they affirmed a woman's worth in the literary marketplace.

Now that I'm retired, I can devote more time to writing. After having struggled for respect as a woman in the workplace, and having experienced the heartache of being both divorced and widowed, I find that writing has once again become a cathartic exercise for me.

In my "retirement," and in my sixties and seventies, I managed to publish five mystery novels. I pour my passion for writing into my characters. Like poems, they are metaphors for love and loss.

In one story, my woman detective works for an ambitious bank manager and solves the murder of one of his employees. In another, I focus on a man who must choose between his girlfriend (our detective) and his daughter. For me, the work that

A LOVELY LIGHT

Maryellen Winkler

detectives do to solve crimes reflects the struggle we all face in solving life's problems. And best of all? At the end of a mystery novel, justice is served.

During the 2021 Super Bowl, as I watched Amanda Gorman recite "Chorus of Captains," I was filled with pride and appreciation for her talent as a writer. I was also hyperaware of all the obstacles she conquered before standing on that stage, not the least of which were gender, age, and race. Writers know that as difficult as it is to write well, the writing may be the least challenging part of the process. After the writing comes editing, publishing, marketing and sometimes reciting your work in front of an audience. I was surprised to learn, after listening to an interview with Gorman, that she struggled with a speech impediment; who would have guessed this when her performances are so strong and beautifully enunciated?

Women writers in 2021 need not be concerned with whether or not they can compete with men. We are finally recognized, published, interviewed, and in

A LOVELY LIGHT

Maryellen Winkler

the public eye more than ever. I'm grateful to have lived long enough to see these changes for women writers, because Amanda Gorman is a lovely light for us all to witness and cherish. At just 22 years of age, she became the youngest inaugural poet in U.S. history. Listening to "Chorus of Captains," I was moved and inspired in the same ways I was as a teenager. Hearing her insight and passion, expressed in rhythm and words, I felt the truth of poetry in my soul again.

Amanda Gorman has inspired me to revisit some of my old, unfinished poems and enroll in a poetry workshop with Osher Lifelong Learning Institute. Thank you, Amanda, for reminding me what a pleasure and a blessing good poetry is.

Made in the USA
Middletown, DE
12 May 2021